Trails and
Michigan Back Roads
by
Ron Rademacher

Have Fun
Ron

Revised Edition

Back Roads Publications
P.O. Box 168
Hart, Michigan 49420

Page Numbers Map

TABLE OF CONTENTS

Trails and Treasures
Michigan Back Roads

by

Ron Rademacher

Back Roads Publication
P. O. Box 168
Hart, Michigan 49420

Acknowledgments

Cover Photograph – Union Mine Trail
Cover photograph by Ron Rademacher

Thanks are due to all the folks in the small Michigan towns who have made time for my presentations, endless questions, and photographic intrusions.

A special thanks to the shops and businesses who supported and sponsored this project.

Proofreading by Kathy Jacobs.

Trails and Treasures
Michigan Back Roads

by Ron Rademacher

Published by
Back Roads Publications
P.O. Box 168
Hart, Michigan 49420

ISBN: 978-0-9883138-2-8

Au Sable River Highbanks Trail

World famous for trout fishing, the Au Sable River, runs more than 100 miles through some of the most beautiful wilderness in lower Michigan before flowing into Lake Huron. Far up atop the bluffs along the river, the *Au Sable Highbanks Trail*, affords some of the most spectacular scenic views in Northern Michigan. The trail runs some seven miles along the Au Sable River Valley. There are access points to this ski/hike trail, 15 miles outside of Oscoda, at Iargo Springs and the Lumberman's Monument. In the height of the season, these areas will often be crowded with tourists. The noise of people and traffic tend to diminish the experience to be found in this beautiful wilderness. However, there is an uncrowded spot, where you can access one of the most beautiful sections of the high banks, and enjoy a short walk along the bluffs.

You can park at the junction of the Au Sable Road and USFS Road 3993, to avoid driving on gravel, and walk in, or you can drive in on 3993 to the parking area. If you decide to walk in, you will immediately enter the towering pines and mixed hardwood trees, of the Huron National Forest. The path to the bluffs isn't very long and it will only take a short time to reach the split rail fence that runs along this section of the Highbanks Trail. The fence runs along an overlook that is more than 100 feet above the river.

At the overlook you can simply pause, rest and take in the breathtaking view of the bend in the Au Sable River, spread out below. A gentle pathway runs along the top of the bluff in both directions for short distances to get even more perspectives on the river valley. Needless to say, this is a spot cherished by photographers during color tour time. For the adventurous, and those in good physical condition, there is a stairway that winds down the bluff all the way to the river. It is a long way down, but well worth it if you have the energy. During the warm months you may well encounter hikers doing the whole seven miles, also fishermen and paddlers on the river. In the winter, you might be the only person there, taking in the pure air, high up on the bluffs.

Local Treasures:

Iargo Springs is easily one of the most beautiful, and easily missed, spots in Northeast Michigan. Far down the cliff are pools of pristine spring waters, that have been visited and revered since humans first found the springs, in the distant past. These ancient springs form large pools of crystal clear water.   The water is so perfectly transparent that you can easily see all the way down to the floor of the pool. When you visit Iargo Springs you will need to be prepared to handle the steps, some 300 of them, take your time. There are several places on the stairs to pause, rest and enjoy the view. Keep your eye peeled for the Bald Eagles that live here.

The springs are just one of the stops along the *River Road Scenic Byway* which runs 22 miles along the Au Sable River. This drive begins at the junction with U.S. 23 in Iosco County, and is one of two National Scenic

Byways, in Michigan. The road winds through the forest that is home to a variety of wildlife, including the occasional black bear. The scenery is gorgeous in all four seasons. You will be treated to breathtaking views from the high river banks and Iargo Springs is just a short distance off the main track. There are six dams in this section of the river, and there are several attractions to visit including the Lumberman's Monument.

Bird watchers will want to drive route F-32 from the Au Sable Road to Mio. The drive winds along the course of the river through *Kirtland's Warbler* country. There are a couple of viewing spots on this route with interpretive signs explaining the habitat. From Mio, you can access the Jack Pine Auto Tour, a self-guided drive through a very special part of Oscoda County in Northern Michigan. This jack pines area attracts the Kirtland's Warbler due to improved eco-system management. The drive is enhanced by interpretive signs along the way that explain the unique methods required to produce habitat that will attract this once endangered species. Some of the stops along the way include clear-cuts, planned burn areas and at least one nature walk.

There is much more to explore in this area. The innkeepers at the *Pines B&B* in Glennie know all of the hidden treasures in the region. Whether you are hiking, camping, fishing, or tubing, you will probably need some supplies. You can find maps, guidebooks and every gadget imaginable at the *Mio Ace Hardware* in downtown Mio. The sponsorship of both of these locally owned Michigan businesses, made this chapter possible.

Directions:

There are a couple of ways to get to the short section of the Highbanks Trail.

From **Mio** - Go north on Route 33 a short distance out of town you will cross the Au Sable River. The next turn to the east is F-32 to McKinley. In a few miles you can go north or south. Go south toward Glennie. In about a mile, will be a turn to the west, USFS 3993, to the Highbanks Overlook.

From Route 65 at **Glennie** or Curan, take the route west toward the Alcona Dam Pond to reach the same spot. F-32 McKinley Road to the Au Sable Road to USFS Road 3993 or Route 65 to the junction at the Glennie Road in Glennie. That road west from Glennie is called the Bamfield Road and will go to the Au Sable Road.

Important Notes:

The Au Sable Highbanks Trail is open year-round. There is no fee required to use the trail.

Barney's Lake Trail

Beaver Island, in Lake Michigan, is the largest island in the archipelago and is known as the Jewel of the Great Lakes and, also, America's Emerald Isle. The interior of the island holds a treasure trove of historic and natural destinations. One of the most popular, for an easy hike, bird watching, and even a little fishing, is the trail network at the *Barney's Lake Nature Preserve*. The trails, which include old logging and farming tracks, take you through a surprisingly rich variety of habitats for such a small area. Managed by the Little Traverse Conservancy, habitats include open meadows, hardwood forest, sedge meadows, and cedar swamp. The trail begins in an open meadow that once held the homestead of Barney O'Donnell's farm. The buildings are gone, but in their place are huge lilac bushes. The meadow is also home to an expanse of milkweed; expect to encounter some of the 40+ species of butterflies found here, including migrating monarchs, in late autumn. The pathway leads into the old orchard, and to a fork in the trail, where the first signpost is located. Various loops can be taken through a total of about 1 ½ miles with only gentle elevation changes.

These trails have become an important stop on the Beaver Island Birding Trail, due to the amazing numbers and varieties of birds. The abandoned farm fields now contain a mix of plant life that supports all manner of insects. The insects provide the food supply the birds require after the exertion of long migratory flights.

Common Loons can be seen on the lake. Bald Eagles and ospreys can be seen hunting in the skies above. There has recently been an osprey nest high up in a nearby cell tower. The marshy areas attract sandpipers, warblers, thrushes, and American Bitterns. The mix of low shrubs and wildflowers along the trails attract a dozen different song birds.

Local Treasures:

Maps showing the location of Barney's Lake, and other birding sights, can be obtained from the ***Beaver Island Birding Trail Association***. This organization has developed several trails on the island, with an excellent system of signage showing the way, and describing the dozens of species of birds to be found here. There are even sites dedicated to attracting birds into town. On the grounds of the Government Building, a ***Chimney Swift Tower*** has been constructed. Most of the old masonry chimneys that were home to these "flying cigars" have disappeared. The construction of these towers provides nesting sites for a species that could face extinction without them.

The ***Beaver Island Archipelago*** is comprised of several islands each with distinctive characteristics. In addition to Beaver Island, there is High Island, a favorite for bird watchers, Whiskey Island, Squaw Island, with its iconic lighthouse, now abandoned, Garden Island is famous for morel mushrooms, Trout Island, Hog Island is known for the fishing, Gull Island is where the birding bay is located, and there are the North and South Fox islands.

The unique history of Beaver Island is preserved at the *Historical Museums*. There have been several distinct historical eras on the island, identified by the people who settled there including Native Americans, a Mormon group with King Strang as its leader and Irish immigrants. The rich heritage of all of the groups, is chronicled and preserved at the museums. The Historical Society manages two museums, the Print Shop Museum and the Marine Museum, as well as two additional historical sites, Heritage Park and the Protar Home.

A Bit of History:

Feodor Protar, a scholar, actor and publisher from Estonia emigrated to America, and then came to Beaver Island in 1893. At that time, there was no doctor on the island. Protar who was not a physician took on the role of healer, caring for patients and dispensing medicine until his death in 1925. *Protar's Tomb*, and his home, are a few miles outside of town on Sloptown Rd. Due to his humanitarian work, and selfless attention to the less fortunate, he became a beloved figure. He was known for his generosity, in that he never required payment for his services, from those who were impoverished, and he never discriminated. His home, built of massive hand-hewn cedar logs, has been preserved and is open to visitors a few times each year.

Directions:

From the Port of St. James, take Kings Highway south 1¼ miles to Barney's Lake Rd. North. Turn right and continue 2½ miles. The Barney's Lake Preserve is on both sides of the road. The parking area is marked by a sign.

You can get to Beaver Island by lake ferry if you need to take equipment or a car and have time for the 2-3 hour trip. A convenient way to go is the 20 minute flight provided by our sponsor, *Island Airways*.

Important Notes:

Many of the destinations on the island are in the wilderness on dirt roads or two track trails. Another important thing to remember is that, though you may be just few miles out of town, you could very likely be off the grid.

Traveling to Beaver Island is part of the adventure. The car ferry can get you there in a couple of hours, depending on conditions on Lake Michigan. If you are in a hurry to get there, our sponsor, *Island Airways*, can whisk you across the lake to the island in about 20 minutes. The flight is great, with views of the lake below and, the scenery of the entire island visible during the trip.

Beach To Beach Trail

We often think that the best trails are far out in the wilderness. In many cases, that is true, but there are any number of excellent trails in urban areas. One of the most popular urban trails in Northern Michigan, is the section of the Betsie Valley Trail, known to the birdwatchers as the *Beach to Beach Trail*. Not only is it a beautiful walk along the lake, there are probably more bird species here than most any other similar trail. The Benzie Audobon Club, has recorded more than 250 species of birds.

The trail is paved most of the way, so expect to find some bicycles and other nature lovers on wheels. From Mineral Springs Park in Frankfort, the trail heads east along the shoreline of Betsie Lake with a short bend around the city docks, and then south along the lake again. It is not unusual to hear the beautiful song of the Warbling Vireo along this trail. All manner of waterfowl will be on the lake, including swans most times of the year. If you cross M-22 at the southern end of the trail past the lake, you can ascend the Audubon platform for a panoramic view of the extensive marshes along the Betsie River.

From this point there are several options. You can make your way back to town and on to the beach at Lake Michigan. You could continue on along the Betsie Valley Trail, to any number of scenic locations. If you are looking for a spectacular view of the Betsie Valley and Lake Michigan, the *Elberta Bluffs* are the place to head for. The overlook is off of Bye Street in Elberta. It offers an unrivaled view of the lake, breakwaters, and Elberta Beach. From the overlook area, you can either drive, or, walk down a very steep narrow path to Elberta Beach. To get to the Elberta Bluffs, you have to follow Furnace Ave. along the waterfront in Elberta to Bye St.

Local Treasures:

The ***Frankfort Lighthouse***, located on the north breakwater in the harbor at the end of Forest Ave., was first lit in 1873. The lighthouse seen today was constructed in 1912, and was added to the National Register of Historic Places in 2005.

The oldest standing structure in Benzie County is the ***Point Betsie Lighthouse,*** built in 1858. About five miles north of Frankfort and west of Beulah, the lighthouse stands adjacent to a public beach, consequently, it is easy to get to and has become one of the most photographed lighthouses in America. Standing at the southern end of the Manitou Passage, the light remains in use as a navigational aid. The lighthouse is open for tours on weekends, from Memorial Day to Columbus Day, with parking at the site.

For a bit of shopping and the best coffee around, head on over to ***Petals & Perks*** in downtown Frankfort. The store is located across from the marina, in one of the oldest buildings in Frankfort, the former Classens Department Store. During the renovations the original hardwood floors were uncovered, and some of the original brick walls were exposed to help create a one-of-a-kind coffee shop atmosphere. Petals and Perks offers free Wi-Fi and several seating areas, even a semi-private room, perfect for a small group meeting.

When I am in this area, I try to have at least one meal at the *Cabbage Shed,* in Elberta. George A. Douglas built the town's first general merchandise store on this site in 1867, thus the motto, "We were here before you were born." It was in the 1930's, when the warehouse was stacked floor to ceiling with cabbage for shipment by rail, that it came to be known as the "Cabbage Shed." The food is consistently very good, and you can find items on the menu that you won't find anywhere else, like their delicious borscht.

A Bit of History:

One branch of the Betsie valley Trail, will take you to Crystal Lake and the Village of Beulah. It was here that an event known as the *"Mistake on the Lake"* occurred. Archibald Jones owned a shipping business here back in the 1870's. He decided that he could improve that business by connecting Crystal Lake and Lake Michigan. He set about digging a canal without checking for elevation differences between the two bodies of water. When the canal was completed, and the lakes connected, the water level in Crystal Lake plunged. As a result, there is now waterfront property all around Crystal Lake, and the Village of Beulah was settled. To commemorate the event, the Village of Beulah hosts the annual

"Archibald Jones Day" festival every Autumn.

Directions:

Parking for the Beach to Beach Trail is available on the waterfront in Frankfort, at Mineral Springs Park, just a few blocks from the beach at Lake Michigan.

Important Notes:

From the Audubon Platform to the Elberta Bluffs is quite a distance. You may want to return to Frankfort first, and drive to the overlook.

Beal Plantation Trail

By the late 1800s, the lumberjacks had cleared the forests near Grayling, leaving little more than pine stumps as far as the eye could see. In those years, no one knew how to replant a forest, it had never been done. Professor W.J. Beal, took matters in hand, and planted more than 40 species of trees in establishing the Grayling Experimental Station. The *Beal Plantation Trail* winds through what may be the oldest documented tree plantation in North America. The trail includes interpretive signs describing the trees, grasses, and clovers that were all part of the experiment, to determine how to reforest these poor sandy soils.

The short walk through the Beal Plantation, is a tour of all that remains of 80 acres planted in 1888. A walk along this trail is a walk through forestry history. As an educational experience, this hike is hard to beat. The variety of trees that can be studied in a short walk, is unmatched anywhere in Northern Michigan.

Local Treasures:

One can hardly consider the forests of Grayling, without mentioning the Old Growth Trail at *Hartwick Pines*. Hartwick Pines State Park, is the largest state park in the lower peninsula of Michigan, encompassing more than 9,000 acres. The most unique feature of the park is a 49 acre stand of Old Growth Pines. These Old Growth Pines provide a living reminder of the splendor of the past, and the importance of lumbering to Michigan. As you stroll beneath the tall pines, the needles on the ground silence your footsteps. In fact, silence will envelope you and, along with the scents and whispering breeze, will refresh you in no time at all. The Logging Muscum is located along the Old Growth Foot Trail, and is open May 1 through October 31.

Tip'N The Mitten, sponsor of this chapter, is much more than just your average store. They focus solely on only those products which are Michigan-made. Owned and operated by Michiganders, everything in this shop from food, to books, to gifts, and more, is made and/or designed in Michigan. Thanks to Tip'n the Mitten, Grayling residents and visitors have access to the best Michigan-made products, all in one place! You will find the new and the tried and true brands that you have come to know and love, and gift items from folks you may not have discovered yet. Store policy is, "If we don't love, we don't sell it".

While you are in downtown Grayling, there are a couple of other stops that are "must see", and both involve food, so try to be hungry. One is the *Classic 50's Diner,* across the street from Tip'n the Mitten. The food is good and the diner is home to the Bottle-Cap Museum which, at 10,000+ pieces, is the largest private collection of Coca-Cola related items in Northern Michigan.

The second, Spikes Keg O' Nails, is known as the "meeting place of the north". This restaurant has been a favorite for generations of visitors in all seasons. The "Spike Burger", is one of my top three burgers in the entire state of Michigan.

Just outside of town is another hidden treasure. ***Wellington Farm Park,*** is a place frozen in time, where it is always 1932. Wellington Farm was an actual community in Northern Michigan. Farming was the main activity between the 1880s and the early 1900s. In 1918 the post office was closed, and those services were provided by the post office in Grayling. When that happened, the people began to move away, and all that remained were a few farm buildings. Today, Wellington Farm USA Park, described as a 60-acre open-air interpretive museum, gives visitors a chance to experience life as it was in rural America during the Great Depression. The park contains a Blacksmith Shop, Grist Mill, Sawmill, Carpenter's Shop, Machine Shed, Farmer's Market, Summer Kitchen and Barnyard. All of the shops are functional, and have restored and authentic equipment inside. During the season, based on availability, craftsmen are in these shops doing the work in the same way, and with the same tools, as in the 1930s.

Important Notes:

The Beal Plantation is handicapped accessible and offers a self guided tour.

THE

GRAYLING

WAS

KNOWN

AS THE

LADY

OF

THE

STREAM

Bear River Valley Trail

Of all the urban trails in Michigan, the pathway through the *Bear River Valley* stands alone, for variety and beauty. The Bear River begins its winding course at Walloon Lake, before it splits the city of Petoskey, ending as a small waterfall on the water front at Little Traverse Bay. This trail follows the course of the river, from the Lake Street Bridge to the Standish Ave Bridge, for a bit over a mile and has any number of recreational opportunities. It may be named bear, but this trail is as gentle as a lamb.

The pathway is quite wide and paved. The trail winds along the river through steep bluffs and forested hills, with several overlooks. There are wide grassy areas to pause for a picnic, and there are benches and convenience facilities as well. After rounding the first bend in the trail, it is hard to believe that this gorgeous spot is in the middle of a city. The paved trail is so smooth, that in the warm months it is popular with moms with strollers and other nature lovers on wheels. In the winter, you might want to bring snowshoes.

If you begin at the Lake Street end, you are only a couple of blocks from downtown Petoskey. The gazebo here is popular with bird watchers, and those who like to watch the fishermen. Within just a short walk you enter the fairly deep gorge created by the river. This river was once a gentle stream flowing sedately to the bay. A few man-made changes, like the addition of large boulders, ledges, logs and tight squeezes have transformed it into a whitewater course unlike anything else in lower Michigan. In May and June, the Bear River is high, and the water churns and boils as it plunges and roars just a few feet from the paved pathway. Watching the kayaks rip along is great fun for young and old.

As beautiful as the Bear River Trail is, it can be crowded in the tourist season. If a quiet stroll on shaded trails, through towering trees is what you are after, the *Trails at Bay View* is the place to go. Just a short walk from the parking area, is the entrance to the Gateway Trail, enter there and you are in an old forest. Bay View, is an historic community on the north side of Petoskey, overlooking Little Traverse Bay. The 400+ cottages have been there since the late 1800s. In 1988, the cottages were designated as a National Historic Landmark, only the 17th such site in the state of Michigan. Tucked away behind the homes, is a system of trails that even many locals don't know about. Winding pathways take you through the forest, where mushrooms and wildflowers grow. Birdwatchers love these trees, and it is a favorite spot for walking the dogs. There is also a steep hill for the adventurous.

Local Treasures:

If you want to take a short hike of a completely different kind, try the *Petoskey Community Labyrinth*. Located on the grounds of the Petoskey District Library, the labyrinth, thirty five feet in diameter, is of the medieval, 11 circuit "Breamore" style, and is open to the public all year.

The Petoskey Gaslight District is a shoppers paradise, with a remarkable variety of shops and galleries. All this hiking, walking, and shopping tends to build an appetite. There are a dozen great places to eat. An historic favorite is the City Park Grill, famous for the 32 foot solid mahogany bar where Ernest Hemingway worked on story notes.

A Bit of History:

In 1917, Prohibition was passed into law in Michigan. The owner of the City Park Grill was having none of it. He built secret underground tunnels to the Cushman Hotel, and the Grill Café to export alcohol. These tunnels are no longer in existence because of sewers and other city infrastructure, but the doors and openings are still there, down in the basement.

Directions:

To get to the ***Bay View Trails,*** take US 31 north to MacDonald Dr. where Kilwin's is. Turn right and take the first left on to Arlington Ave. Follow that to the stop sign, go straight through, and keep going until you see the tennis courts on your right. Park at the tennis courts, and walk past them on the left. The entrance to the Gateway Path is just past the courts.

THE

LEWISTON

CURLING

CLUB

IS

AVAILABLE

TO THE

PUBLIC

Beaver Pond Trail

The Beaver Pond Trail is unusual in several ways. It is just a side loop off another trail. It is within the boundaries of the *Fiborn Karst Preserve* and it provides a view that is unlike any other that I know of in Michigan. The Fiborn Karst Preserve covers nearly 500 acres. The area was the site of a limestone quarry that operated in the early 1900s supplying Algoma Steel of Sault Ste. Marie, Ontario. The abandoned quarry is a popular destination for hikers and history buffs. In the middle of the quarry are the ruins of the railroad house and the ore car loader.

This is a karst formation which means that there are sinkholes, springs and caves formed by running water. The streams and swamps drain into the Hendrie River, dissolving the limestone as the water flows. Another unique feature of this area is the *Hendrie River Water Cave*. It is the longest known cave in Michigan and has a stream running through it. The cave is narrow, difficult, and considered dangerous. Entry is restricted requiring a guide and a permit. Other caves exist in the area. All are wet and unsuitable for amateur explorations.

Fortunately, other features of the preserve can be enjoyed safely in all seasons thanks to the trails that are maintained there. The trailhead is found at the information kiosk where a simple map brochure is available. The Sinkhole Trail is a short loop that passes by shallow sinkholes and takes visitors to a creek that disappears below ground. The ***Ann Patrie Memorial Trail*** is longer, about one and a half miles. It skirts the edge of the quarry through second-growth forest, sinkholes and crevasses and eventually offers entry into the far end of the quarry. It is along the Ann Patrie trail where the Beaver Pond Trail loop is found.

The Beaver Pond Trail is marked by a small sign. The trail is a bit rough and has some difficult parts due to thick foliage and steep grades. Fortunately, the difficult parts are short and lead the hiker to the edge of hill that is steep enough to be regarded as a cliff. Standing on the edge of the precipice you are a couple hundred feet above a vast wetland that stretches at least a half mile into the distance. The swampy wetland is crisscrossed by several streams that eventually combine into a small river. It at this point that the area gets its name. Across the breadth of the river is an enormous Beaver Dam. The sight of the dam, the vast wetland dotted with beaver mounds and the wild forest in the distance make this a scene that one would expect to find only in the Canadian wilderness or the western mountains of America.

Getting There; The Fiborn Karst Preserve is west of Trout Lake. Take route 40 west about 5 or 6 miles. After you cross a very small bridge the Quarry Road will take you north to the quarry and information kiosk. The Quarry Road is rough gravel.

Buttles Road Pathway

Montmorency County, east of Gaylord, is known for its snowmobile trails, ice fishing, and hunting. Consulting a map, one can see little in the way of hiking trails. There is one that is excellent in any season but is especially beautiful in the winter. That is the *Buttles Road Pathway*.

One description I saw mentioned that, since the trails are in fairly open areas, it should be avoided on windy winter days. That opinion is pure horse-pucky, if you ask me. Winter hiking and skiing requires care and preparation. These trails are gorgeous in the winter, and the sound of the wind through the oaks, pines, and birches is mesmerizing. The silence in the forest, can make you pause, just to listen, the sound of the wind in the trees is beautiful. This is a fine walk in any season; in winter the solitude is awesome.

Buttles is a hiking and cross-country ski path only, no snow machines. The trail head is immediately off the parking area. The main loop is about six and one-half miles. At the far end, the trail skirts two remote lakes, Crystal Lake and Hidden Lake. There are two other loops. One is about one mile and the other is just under two miles. The shortest loop branches to the north and is mostly flat terrain. That loop is a great place to hike with snowshoes. The middle loop has moderate, gentle hills and some flat land. It branches off to the left and immediately begins to descend into a grove of pines. If you take the long loop, you will go through all kinds of trees, low hills, and plains.

At the junction for the first two loops is a vault toilet. That's it for facilities, so bring what you need. If you plan to ski, be aware that these trails are not groomed.

Local Treasures:

The *Lewiston Curling Club* is a state of the art curling facility, just three miles from the trail. It is a fun day to hike the trails and then join in some fun at the Curling Club. They have two curling courts, instruction, and all of the equipment. Reservations are required.

If you want to explore the lakes and snowmobile trails, the *Lewiston Hotel* welcomes sportsmen. They can handle large groups, pet friendly and make one of the best burgers in Michigan.

Directions:

The trail head parking lot is on Buttles Road between M-32 and County Road 612 in Lewiston.

Chippewa Arbury Trail

The Chippewa Nature Center in Midland, Michigan has more than 15 miles of trails that are free and open to the public. A special trail at the nature center is the ***Arbury Trail***. It is a paved loop of less than half a mile and is ideal for nature lovers of limited mobility. You can actually enter the trail directly from the parking lot. Along this easy walking pathway are four different ecosystems under management. Included on this fun little hike is an overlook of the Pine River. There are few ***"special use"*** trails that are as enjoyable as this one. At the conclusion of the loop, you are right back at the parking area and can go on your way or, take a few minutes and tour the beautiful visitors center.

There are several other trails at the nature center. All of them take the hiker through different and diverse habitats. Among the trails available there is the "Chippewa Trail" that runs from the nature center, through the forests and wetlands for 3.5 miles to the "Tridge" in downtown Midland. There is the "River Trail" that follows the course of the river and is also groomed for cross country skiing. The "Wetlands Trail" is a couple of minutes from the nature center. It is about a mile and a half long and covers all of the nature center wetland types. The board walks and docks make for an easy and dry walk through the wetlands.

On all of these trails wildlife abounds. Since there is a river and wetlands, water loving species like kingfishers, pileated woodpeckers, wood ducks, and warblers are here along with the eagles and hawks. In addition to the birds, observant hikers may see river otters and mink.

Local Treasures:

Downtown Midland is connected to the nature center via the Chippewa Trail. Distinctive shops like the Coyer Candle Company and a local winery, Grape Beginnings, are just two of the stops to enjoy while touring the *Tridge* and the Santa House.

Every year in May, the garden known as the *Dahlia Hill* is recreated in Midland. The hill consists of eight terraces that showcase 3,000+ dahlias including over 250 varieties. There are three stairways that go up the hill. Take anyone of them and you will quickly be surrounded by the dahlias. Gravel pathways wind along the stone terraces. Each variety of dahlia is there with labels to help with identification.

Scattered throughout are garden sculptures created by artist Charles Breed. These works are representations of the cycles of life and the seasons. Benches and resting areas are located near the parking area and at the top terrace. All of this is the work of The Dahlia Hill Society. Their goal is to grow show-quality dahlias in a garden setting. The museums on top of Dahlia Hill contain the original artwork of Charles Breed. Most of the art is based on botanical and floral shapes.

Alden B. Dow House - Midland is a town that is full of beautiful architecture and nature areas. On the grounds of the Dow Botanical Gardens is the ***Alden B. Dow*** house, notable even in a community that is full of historic buildings. Alden B. Dow, son of Dow Chemical founder, Herbert H. Dow, was an architectural artist. The home and studio he created are considered a masterpiece of quality and originality. Among other creations, this work earned him lasting national recognition. The geometric lines of the house somehow blend easily into the surrounding gardens and water features. The sunken conference room inside actually sits below the water level. The house remains an extraordinary example of modern 20th century design. The house is open to the public. The Dow Gardens cover more than 100 acres and have been in continuous development since 1899.

A Bit of History:

There is another trail that deserves a mention, the ***Midland to Mackinac*** trail. For hundreds of years, this trail was used by Native Americans as a seasonal path for hunting, trapping, and general travel. Today the trail simulates the original route as it weaves through forests and and meadows. This trail has few improvements and does not provide a return loop so you have to retrace your steps. Following the route of the historic Mackinac Pathway, the trail stretches from Midland to Mackinaw City.

Directions:

Chippewa Nature Center from downtown Midland, take Hwy. west 20 to S. Homer Rd., go south to E. Prairie

Road, go east to S. Badour Road.

Midland To Mackinac Au Sable State Forest Trailhead:
Take M-30 north about 8 - 10 miles. Turn right onto
Shearer Road. Travel several miles east to trail head
parking on left hand side of road.

Important Notes:

The Chippewa Nature Center trails are open dawn to
dusk. The Arbury Trail is wheelchair accessible directly
from the park area.

Dark Sky Trails

Michigan made history at Lake Hudson in the 1990's, when it became the first state in the US to protect land, for the quality of its dark sky. Far to the north in Emmet County, they took this idea to the ultimate level and created the *Headlands Dark Sky Park* which meets the criteria of the International Dark Sky Association. Upon being designated a Dark Sky Park in 2011, it was one of only six such parks in the US, and one of 9 in the world at the time.

The Headlands consists of 600 acres of old-growth forest, several trails, and about 2 ½ miles of Lake Michigan Shoreline. There are more than four miles of easy trails, in several loops, from less than half a mile up to two miles. There is also a self-guided, via cell phone, Dark Sky Discovery trail. All trails are accessible from the main parking area. In addition to the trails, about a quarter of a mile of shoreline, in a quiet cove on Lake Michigan is available to trail users. All of this area has been protected specifically for nighttime star gazing.

Dark Sky Parks and other protected public lands offer exceptional opportunities for star gazing in a natural nocturnal environment. As of 2014 there were only twelve Dark Sky Parks in the world with nine of them in the U.S.

Local Treasures:

Directly across from the Dark Sky entrance, is the *Mackinaw Historical Society Heritage Village*. The complex consists of a variety of historic structures from about 1880 through 1917. This was a period of dramatic changes in transportation, communication, housing, health care, and nearly every other aspect of life. The village covers about 140 acres with lots of unique and one-of-a-kind buildings. The bone room is a small kiosk with hands on displays that will fascinate kids of all ages. The last existing Pestilence House in Michigan is part of the village. A Pestilence House is a quarantine facility that was found in nearly every Michigan community around 1900. This example was built in the 1890s, and was rediscovered in 2004, in the form of a long-deserted machine shop. These houses were used to quarantine individuals who became infected with dangerous contagious diseases like diphtheria, cholera, and smallpox. Advances in medical treatment made Pestilence Houses obsolete. They deteriorated and fell apart or were dismantled and destroyed. This is the only one I have found that survived, and that has been fully restored.

Less than a mile north of the Heritage Village is the *McGulpin Point Lighthouse*. It is an example of a true lighthouse, with a light tower and attached lighthouse keeper's living quarters. It was built in 1869 and operated until 1906. The design, called Norman Gothic, was so successful it was used in at least three other lighthouses including, the Eagle Harbor Light, White

River Light, and Sand Island Light.

Down the hill from the lighthouse is the **McGulpin Rock,** on the shore of Lake Michigan, at McGulpin Point. The big rock has been used as a navigational aid for centuries. The McGulpin Rock is about five times the size of the more famous Plymouth Rock. French explorers in the 1600's used it to gauge water levels. Native Americans had used it for centuries before that.

If you plan to drive the **Tunnel of Trees** be sure to visit the **Cross Village General Store,** for essential goodies, like hand-dipped ice cream cones. In 1999, The Howard Family, resurrected the Cross Village General Store in its current location – the first commercial building built in Cross Village since the 1920s. Back by popular demand – giant hand-dipped ice cream cones – a Lee Howard tradition in the village. They have a great deli, cold drinks, Michigan gifts, and this is the only place to refuel for miles and miles.

Directions:

The International Dark Sky Park is located about two miles west of downtown Mackinaw City in northwest lower Michigan. From downtown Mackinaw City, head west on Central Avenue, the main street through the downtown. Take it as far as it goes, to the T-intersection at Headlands Road. Turn left, or south, on Headlands Road and watch for the sign on the right.

Important Notes:

At the Headlands - No white light, no fires and no
smoking, no camping, though you can stay out all night
to watch the stars on a blanket or a camp chair. Dogs are
welcome on leashes. Noise should be kept to a minimum
this is a wilderness habitat.

Earl's Prairie Trail

The Seven Ponds Nature Center has 468 acres of natural splendor, that can be toured, via a number of trails. Along the way you can pause near one of the seven glacial lakes, from which the center takes its name, hike the boardwalks across a cedar swamp and verdant marshes, or chronicle the variety of songbirds and waterfowl, that are so abundant here. After even a brief stop, visitors understand why Seven Ponds is described as a place of extraordinary natural beauty. One feature that sets this nature center apart, is the nine acres known as *Earl's Prairie*. Hundreds of years ago, the dense forests of the eastern North American continent, ended at the wide-open areas of tall grasses and wildflowers, of what is now southern Michigan, Ohio, and Indiana. Nearly all of these prairies are gone, but you can experience one here on the *Earl's Prairie* interpretive trail, at Seven Ponds Nature Center.

The trail through Earl's Prairie is adjacent to the parking area. After a very short walk through the trees, you enter what may appear to be a neglected farm field. Follow the trail and learn about the incredible diversity of this small area, at the designated stops along the way. The variety of life in the prairie is amazing. There are dozens of specialized plants and wildflowers growing here. Many are perennials, some of which can live for decades. Some of the plants have adapted specifically for the prairie environment, like Indian Grass and Goldenrod. Bird watchers can find ground nesting birds here, like the bobolink and eastern meadowlark. These birds are tricky. They conceal the location of their nests by landing some feet away, and then sneak through the tall grass to the actual nest. Another treat along the trail will be the large number of hummingbirds, gathering nectar from the prairie flowers. You may even hear the call of a kingfisher, working away at the Prairie Pond.

The meadow isn't just flowers and weeds. Quiet hikers may very well encounter some of the cottontail rabbits and groundhogs living in the prairie. You may not see them, but the hawks soaring overhead, are a sure sign that field mice and meadow voles are hiding in the thick grass. Another hidden feature of the prairie is the insect population. Look carefully and you can find katydids and walking sticks clinging to the flower stems. The milkweed is where you can find butterflies. It is estimated that there are nearly a million insects in this nine acre area. If you come out early in the morning before the dew has dried, huge areas of the prairie may be festooned with "bowl & doily" webs sparkling in the sunrise, sure evidence of the several species of spiders living here.

There are several informative stops on the trail and an elevated viewing platform. The entire Earl's Prairie trail is about one mile. A trail guide pamphlet is available at the visitors center.

Local Treasures:

The *Butterfly Garden* on the grounds of the Seven Ponds Nature Center exhibits a variety of plants that attract butterflies.

A must see for the kids is ***Watson the Pacu***. He is a huge
freshwater fish, of a species related to the piranha. Even
though his diet is mainly vegetarian, he is BIG. Watson
weighs in at around 60 pounds and is probably three feet
long. Watson isn't just another pretty face. He has a
coloring book dedicated to his life and is well known on
social media. He lives in his aquarium, in the lobby, at
the Oxford Public Library.

The ***White Horse Inn,*** in downtown Metamora, was said
to be haunted in the first century it was in operation. The
inn closed in 2012. It has now been remodeled and is
open again. The food is delicious, and the décor is
breathtaking. No sightings of the ghost have been
reported.

Directions:

Five miles east of Metamora, the nature center and
sanctuary are open all year to members, or by admission
fee.

Important Notes:

Calkins Road is gravel. Seven Ponds Nature Center
charges admission.

EMPIRE

IS

THE

GATEWAY

TO

THE

SLEEPING

BEAR

DUNES

Empire Bluffs Trail

The Sleeping Bear National Lakeshore is a favorite destination for vacationers from all over the world. Most visitors make it a point to hike out to the overlooks of the Sleeping Bear Dunes and most miss an easy walking trail that has some of the best views anywhere on the shoreline, and arguably, the best sunset in the entire region. The ***Empire Bluffs Trail*** is only about a mile and half round-trip, but there is some elevation change, so this is not a perfectly flat trail. Still, the climb is fairly moderate. The gentleman who told me about this trail is 5 feet nine inches tall and weighs in at a cool 350 pounds. He said he has no problems with this trail at all.

What bit of climbing there is, is well worth it, and is made easier by benches that are placed at intervals along the way. In addition to the wildflowers, hardwood trees and wildlife of every kind that are indigenous to the area, there are scenic vistas that are unique to this trail. At the far end of the trail you are more than 400 feet above Lake Michigan, with a large portion of the Sleeping Bear Dunes area spread out below. At this point you are actually above the highest dunes. The view from here would be difficult to find anywhere else. To the south is the Platte Bay where Coho Salmon were first introduced into the Great Lakes. To the north all of South Manitou Island is visible, and also, part of North Manitou Island as well.

Another feature that makes this trail special, is the nearly total absence of light pollution. Just a short time after those spectacular sunsets are over, the stars come out in a brilliance and profusion that you can rarely find on Lake Michigan. The pure darkness here makes this a favorite destination when we have meteor showers. For annual meteor showers, or a prediction of northern lights, you might want to arrive early. This place will be full of families out to enjoy the show.

Local Treasures:

Sleeping Bear Dunes – Many travelers come to this area specifically to hike the dunes. There are several places in the area from which to access the dunes.

Pierce Stocking Scenic Drive - This drive, and the surrounding area, have been called the most beautiful place in America. The drive is just a bit more than 7 miles and is open in the summer months only. Those 7 miles offer up some of the most beautiful over-looks in Michigan. The covered bridge is one of the first features encountered. A pull off is provided, as this is a favorite spot for photography. There are several scenic turn offs and picnic areas. Spectacular views of Lake Michigan, the Manitou Islands and Sleeping Bear Dunes are found all along the way. The Pierce Stocking Drive is located off state highway M-109 between Empire and Glen Arbor.

Port Oneida Historic District – Port Oneida is one of the most unique historic districts in all of Michigan. It doesn't appear on many maps, so it is one of the least visited attractions in the area. Port Oneida grew into a sizable community in the late 1800s, as a result of the lumber industry and the work of Thomas Kelderhouse. Eventually the area included a dock on Lake Michigan, blacksmith shop, post office, general store and a boarding house. The historic farmsteads and some of the buildings have been preserved and can be visited via a scenic drive. *Note: Some of the roads on the drive are gravel.*

One of the most photographed barns in Michigan, on the D. H. Day farmstead, is nearby. The barn, built in the late 1800s, has twin silos and an ogee (bell-shaped) roof with octagonal cupolas topping it all off. You really can't miss it. It doesn't lie in the district but is within the boundaries of the park.

Art's Tavern – Located in downtown Glen Arbor this is a favorite spot for lunch or dinner. The place is a bit retro as is should be; it has been there since 1934. Tim Barr is one of the proprietors. On the rare occasion when he isn't busy, he can tell you all about the destinations and history of this region.

Directions:

Empire is in Northwest Michigan, north of Frankfort and west of Traverse City, at the junction of M-22 and M-72. M-72 going west from M-22 becomes the main street into downtown Empire. Follow that street west a few blocks and you will come to a junction where you must turn, go left. This will become Wilco Road and in just a short drive you will come to the parking area for the Empire Bluff Trail. The park offices, where you can get passes and information, is just east of M-22 on M-72, big building, you can't miss it.

Important Notes:

The *Empire Bluffs Trail* is within the Sleeping Bear Dunes National Lakeshore. A pass is required to make use of the parking area. Passes are available at the Park Headquarters, as well as maps and important information about the local flora and fauna, like poison ivy and bears. The trail is open year-round and is a popular snowshoe trek. Mountain biking is not allowed.

Many roads through the *Port Oneida Historic District* are gravel. Make a quick stop at the ranger station to pick up the Port Oneida booklet that has descriptions of the buildings and a simple map. You'll need the map to find your way around the district.

Haywire Grade Trail

The Haywire Grade Trail was the first rail-trail in Michigan opening in 1970. The grade was originally part of the Manistique & Northwestern Railroad. The railroad hauled white pine timber from logging camps to lumber mills in Manistique.

The trail runs from M-94, south of Shingleton, to the Water Intake Plant in Manistique on a surface of gravel, dirt, and sand; about 33 miles. The multi-use pathway is primarily used by ATV riders in summer and snowmobilers in winter. This is the backbone of the entire Upper Peninsula snowmobile system. Haywire is also open to mountain biking, hiking and horse riding. The trail includes ballast from the old rail bed upon which it runs, making travel difficult for bikes and horses in some spots.

The trail passes through 2nd growth forest across great distances with nothing but towering trees, wildlife, abandoned settlements and solitude. At one point the trail passes by the abandoned Stueben Landing Field deep in the Hiawatha National Forest. Several stops along the trail have interpretive signs describing the structures and activities that were here and are now lost to history. A couple of towns are still in existence from the old days, Stueben for instance, where there is a small store to get supplies.

PARKING - Parking at the north end of the trail, Shingleton, can be tricky. You have to park about a quarter mile from the trail head near the Tanglewood Inn. Parking is no problem at the Manistique end and there are other outdoor opportunities like a ramble on the boardwalk on the shore of Lake Michigan, go fishing at Indian Lake State Park or launch your kayak on the new launch on the Manistique River.

Hidden Lake Gardens Trails

In the southeast part of Michigan is a famous region known as the Irish Hills. There are rolling hills and scenic vistas in the area, making it a very popular destination, in summer and fall. One of the area attractions that draws visitors back, again and again, is Hidden Lake Gardens. There are nine distinct trails within the more than 700 acres. Whether you are looking for wildflowers in the spring, songbirds or just a quiet walk through the oak and hickory forests, there is a trail here for you. There is even a guided auto trail. Trail maps are available at the visitors center.

Some of these trails can be challenging, but two of them are fun for anyone. Near the hidden lake is a *handicapped access trail*. It has its own parking area which puts you right at the trail head. This trail is paved, it is a loop of less than a mile, so you come right back to the parking area, there are benches and scenic vistas along the way. If you are feeling a bit more adventurous, but don't want to encounter steep hills and ravines, the *Munger South Trail* is just the thing. Munger South, is a loop of under two miles, with gentle hills and beautiful scenery. As you wander these trails, you will see that a large portion of Hidden Lake Gardens has been preserved in its undeveloped state. It is common to encounter white-tail deer, wild turkeys and all manner of songbirds along the way.

There are reasons to visit Hidden Lake Gardens in every season of the year. The gardens trails are open in the winter, but if you want a warm experience in the dead of another Michigan winter, *visit the domes*. There are three of them, Temperate, Tropical and Arid. The temperate dome is where bulbs and shrubs are prepared for spring plantings. The tropical dome is filled with palms, flowers, and fountains. The air is warm, humid and heavily scented by the jungle loam and the flowers that abound. The arid dome contains an entire southwest desert environment. Warmth again surrounds you, but this time, it is arid and dry. After even one hour in the domes, you will have forgotten all about the Michigan winter just outside.

Then, there is the *Bonzai Forest*, with numerous potted bonzai trees, arranged as a forest. Some of these trees are said to be more than 100 years old. Outside the visitors center is the *Hosta Hillside,* where the original rock garden was built by the founder, Mr. Fee, in the 1940s. There are more than 800 varieties of Hosta on display. The Hosta Hillside is an Official American Hosta Society Display Garden, so designated in 1995, and was only the second garden in the country to receive this distinction.

Local Treasures:

Local treasures are just a short drive away, in downtown Adrian, Michigan. In a space of a couple of blocks is an historic opera house, fantastic food, and an extraordinary Michigan gift shop. Together with the gardens, these destinations make for a great day trip.

The *Croswell Opera House* has been here since 1866, making it the oldest theater in Michigan. The opera house is one of the oldest continuously operating theaters in the United States, but it has seen some difficult periods. For a number of years it operated as a movie house and in the 1960's its very survival was touch and go. Fortunately, a group of civic-minded citizens got together, purchased the building, and saved this treasure for live theater. The auditorium has been fully restored to its original 19th-century grandeur, seating about 650.

Downtown Adrian contains any number of historic buildings. A genuine architectural jewel is the *Governor Croswell Tea Room,* located in the one hundred year-old Hoefler Building at 125 E. Maumee St. This is a great place for lunch and inspecting the building is well worth it.

Yes, it is a tea room and you can enjoy a genuine High Tea all everyday but there is more than tea. The authentic fare includes Shepherd's Pie and my favorite, The Ploughman's lunch, which the menu describes as a British farmer's midday feast, eaten while in the fields. The menu lists a generous chunk of aged Scottish white cheddar, a boiled egg, a pickled onion, a hunk of warm crusty bread, dill butter, a crispy dill pickle, and a cup of homemade seasonal soup. Just so good.

Don't miss one of the best gift shops in southeast Michigan, *SASS Gift Shop,* 114 E. Maumee St. in downtown Adrian. The sign says, "Fun Things Inside". Those "fun things" are cool gifts, about half of which are

"Made in Michigan". "Made In America" is another theme of the shop. Diane and Joyce, owners, search the markets to find quality American made products. There are gifts for everyone including those pesky men, specialty Michigan food items, art and jewelry by local artists, and a whole lot more. They can give you directions to any place in town.

Directions:

Hidden Lake Gardens is located at 6214 Monroe Rd. just outside Tipton, Michigan. Get to the junction of U.S. 12 and 52. Head south on 52 to 50 and go west toward Tipton. Watch for the signs.

Important Notes:

There is a small entrance fee at Hidden Lake Gardens.

Hunters Point Park Trail

Hunter's Point Park is one of the real treasures in Copper Harbor. Unlike the famous view up on the Brockway Drive and the Estivant Pines, this is a beautiful spot that is often overlooked. After walking the short hiking trail, you can appreciate how beautiful it is.

The point juts out into the harbor and is visible from downtown. There is excellent parking at the trail that gives access to the point and the Lake Superior shoreline. A handicap accessible boardwalk leads from the parking lot to a Lake Superior viewing deck. The trail from the parking area through the interior of the point is a natural walking trail. There isn't much in the way of grooming. The path winds through tall evergreens and eventually ends at the tip of the point. From that spot a small island is visible in the distance. The lighthouse and downtown Copper Harbor can both be seen.

At several points along the way, side trails lead to the shoreline making it easy to leave the main trail and walk along the north shoreline of the point along Lake Superior. The forests and lake views are spectacular. It is hard to believe that you are only a quarter mile from town. The unusual rock formations are volcanic in nature creating a wild scenic landscape. When a lake fog begins to roll in, the shoreline and forest take on a magical appearance. This is a place where you will take a lot of pictures.

Hunter's Point is a last stop for migrating birds before they cross Lake Superior on their way to Canada. Passerines by the thousands "line up" at the point and take flight in the early hours to make the trek across Lake Superior. Passerines are perching songbirds. What sets them apart from other songbirds is their feet which are designed to automatically grip and hang on to a perch. This allows them to roost in trees and sleep without falling to the ground.

There is a small sign on the west end of town pointing the way to the parking area.

Indian Burial Mounds Trail

As recently as the 1950s, travelers on the back roads in Michigan, could spot old burial mounds left by bands of Native Americans. In Clinton County, there was a bread loaf shaped mound, just east of the corner of Airport Road and Howe Road that was visible from the roadway. Likewise, those traveling on small rivers and streams, were likely to encounter these ancient burial sites. That part of Clinton County, through which flows the Maple River and its tributary creeks, contained a greater number of mounds than any other equal area in the state, except Newaygo County. Nearly all of these sacred spots have been lost due to agricultural activities or community development. There are a few burial mounds that have been preserved and a few have even survived by happenstance. A handful of those mounds can be found in the Rose Lake State Wildlife Nature Preserve.

Referred to locally as Rose Lake, the main entrance to this site is on Stoll Road. The nature preserve encompasses more than 4,000 acres of diverse habitat, wildlife, lakes, streams, and miles of trails. In addition to the main entrance, there are numerous other access points on several local roads. The entrance to what we call the *Indian Mound Trail* is found on Clark Road, in the extreme northwest corner of the preserve.

The trail is unimproved, but it is an easy walk, with only gentle elevation changes. There are no interpretive signs here, so knowing what to look for will help. After following the trail for a bit over a quarter of a mile, there is a large fallen tree with the root stock facing the trail. This is the best trail marker to alert hikers that the mounds are nearby. As the trail begins to descend, there is a large mound off to the right. As with all of the ancient sites, this one is covered with trees, but the regular shape reveals its true nature. If you climb to the top, you will find a broad depression in the ground, indicating that the burial chamber below has collapsed, and the fill dirt has settled.

If you turn, and face back the way you came, you can see the *effigy mound* that most hikers never notice as they walk toward the hill mound. Effigy mounds are rare in Michigan. This one is fairly large, being more than 70 feet long. The mound is in the shape of a salamander with head, four legs, and a tail. The tail is pointing down the trail we came in on, toward Chandler Swamp. This mound is difficult to make out if there is any undergrowth at all. The area is a heavily wooded and is divided by Mud Creek and the Chandler Swamp. Unless one has learned what to look for, the mounds can be extremely difficult to distinguish in the dense undergrowth. Consequently, to even see the mounds, it is best to go in early spring or in the fall after a hard frost, when there is little ground cover.

From this spot the trail continues down a gentle slope to Chandler Marsh. Things get a little messier here, so be forewarned, it is called a marsh, but it acts like a swamp. If you follow the trail through the marsh you will arrive at Mud Creek, where there is usually a small log bridge. Cross the bridge and head at a tangent to the right. Up in the trees are more mounds, one of which is quite large, near the giant oak tree.

The distance from the parking area to Mud Creek, is less than one half mile. This is a forest trail so there are not a lot of wildflowers. The creek and the marsh do attract a wide variety of wildlife and birds. This spot is secluded from the hustle and bustle of the main park area. Even on major weekends, it is not unusual to be completely alone here. The solitude and quiet invite one to pause and listen and be still.

Local Treasures:

After a short walk through the woods it is time to have some fun of a different sort. Take Clark Road back to Old 127. Go south toward Lansing and turn right on Grand River Ave. In just a couple of blocks you will arrive in the historic district know as ***Old Town***. This is a great destination for a little urban hiking. Old Town has been become a favorite destination and, if you go on a weekend, there is very likely to be a festival going on. It's hard to believe that this was once known as the "north side" and was as rough a neighborhood and you could find.

Along with all the shops, galleries, and eateries there are a couple of distinct localities to visit. One is the ***Brenke Fish Ladder,*** which was built in 1981. It was constructed so fish could get around the dam as they head upstream. The fish ladder is a popular place to pause along the Lansing River Trail. There are almost always fishermen nearby, catching catfish, carp, sunfish, and other smaller species of fish. In early autumn this is an excellent place for spotting salmon. Fishing within the ladder is not permitted.

Another distinctive destination, the ***Dodge Mansion***, is also known as Turner-Dodge House. Built in 1855, the Turner-Dodge House is now a museum, preserving the history of Lansing's early pioneers. The style is Classical Revival and this is the only 19th century residence in the region, that is open to the public. The mansion is located at 100 East North Street and is open all year Tuesday – Friday.

A Bit of History:

At one time, there were over 1,000 mounds identified in Michigan, along with numerous enclosures, villages, and garden beds. The part of Clinton County where the Maple River flows, contained more mounds than any area of equal, size except Newaygo County. Effigies were also carved in large and small stone sculptures. These mounds were not scattered randomly across the landscape. They were built along the ancient Indian trails that traverse the state, and along the rivers and streams that served as major highways.

Directions:

The most direct route to the ***Indian Mounds Trail*** entrance is to take Old 127 north out of Lansing to Clark

Rd. There is also an exit to Old 127 from Interstate 69.
Clark Road is just south of the Interstate. Go east for a
few miles and you will arrive in Bath, Michigan. There
is a stop at the junction at Webster Road, continue east.
Go past Upton Road continuing east. After a couple of
hills, there will be a very small parking area, on the north
side of the road, with room for four or five cars. There is
a small marker denoting the trail heading off to the north.
If you come to a curve in the road, you've gone too far.

Important Notes:

This part of the nature preserve is open to hunting, so it is
best to avoid the area during deer hunting season. The
mounds are considered sacred to the local tribes. Please
respect these sites, don't dig, bring out everything you
take in. There are no convenience facilities.

LODA LAKE

WILDFLOWER

SANCTUARY

IS

INSIDE

A

NATIONAL

FOREST

Loda Lake Wildflower Trail

The *Loda Lake Wildflower Sanctuary* is the only wildflower sanctuary inside a National Forest. Through more than 70 acres, and a hiking trail of about 1 1/2 miles, hikers can discover a sampling of wildflower plants that used to cover much of lower Michigan. The Loda Lake Wildflower Sanctuary includes a small spring-fed lake, a wetland area, a creek and marshy areas. There is an oak forest, pine plantations, and the remains of an old farm site. All of this is inside the Manistee National Forest.

This is a beautiful place, and the variety of trails makes it possible to enjoy a stroll through the wildflowers, by trail lovers of all abilities. Loda Lake is in view from the parking area. A short walk along the shoreline brings you to the first wetlands, which you cross on a very well maintained boardwalk. After crossing the wetlands, a right turn will take you to a bench where several trails intersect. One is a loop back to the parking area, another will take you to the pollinator gardens, and the history display. If you turn left after the boardwalk, the trail continues along the lake and eventually loops back through the Red Pine Plantation, and then on to the the history display.

All along the way are wildflowers and native plants. In fact, more than 200 plants have been identified, and you can find them easily, by following the trail map brochures that are provided near the trail head. In addition to the wildflowers there are birds galore. The wildflower sanctuary also has a bird checklist available, that shows more than 120 varieties of birds, to be found in the different habitats. The Loda Lake Wildflower Sanctuary is a gorgeous place for a quiet break or a full day. There is a picnic area and there are rustic restroom facilities. There are no shops.

Local Treasures:

There are all kinds of choices for those who want to make a day of it. In downtown Baldwin, *Jones Homemade Ice Cream* has been a destination for more than 40 years. Some people say it is the best ice cream made in Michigan. *Pandora's Box*, a very cool shop, is right across the street.

The famous *Shrine of the Pines Museum* is also in Baldwin. The Shrine of the Pines is known as a "rustic furniture museum" and sits in a small stand of pines on the famous Pere' Marquette River. The contents of this Michigan treasure are the life work of Raymond W. Overholzer. Inside the log cabin, that serves as the museum, are over 200 pieces of his incredible rustic work. This is the largest collection of rustic pine furniture in the world.

The large dining table was crafted from one white pine stump. It is more than 7 feet across and weighs in excess of 700 pounds. The rocking chair is made mostly of roots. It too, is special. While it may look like other "rustic" rockers you have seen, this one is so well balanced that one push will set it to rocking, and it will keep rocking for more than 50 repetitions. The stunning fireplace is made of 70 tons of stone, there is a wooden gun rack, with 39 wooden ball bearings, and much more.

A Little History:

This area was once a virgin pine forest. The timber was all harvested by the late 1800's, and the land was acquired by the Hanson family of Chicago. A friend, Thomas Hunt, contracted to farm the area, and did so successfully for several years. The Hunts cleared the pine stumps, and planted orchards, and a number of grain crops. In the course of their years here, they constructed homes, an artists studio, barns and other structures. Some of these building sites, orchards and the red pine plantation are marked on the trail by interpretive signs.

After the Hunt family left the area, others tried to continue the farm, but without success. In 1937 the land was declared "sub-marginal" and was sold to the US Forest Service. In 1949 the Michigan Garden Clubs Inc., formed a partnership with the Forest Service. That agreement made the Wildflower Sanctuary we enjoy today possible.

Directions:

The Loda Lake Wildflower Sanctuary is in northern Newaygo County, less than an hour north of Grand Rapids. Take highway M-37, about 6.5 miles north of White Cloud or 18 miles south of Baldwin is 5 Mile Road. Turn west on 5 Mile Road and go follow it to

Felch Road, turn right and go a half mile to the parking area.

Outside of White Cloud is The Shack. This is a great place for people who want to spend the night in the area and continue their explorations the next day.

Important Notes:

Felch Road is gravel.

Lost Mansion Trail

There is a story about a man who, many years ago, wanted to build a mansion atop the majestic sand dunes of Southwest Michigan. While acquiring a site near South Haven, and drawing up building plans, he happened to find a fully constructed stone mansion for sale, across Lake Michigan, near Chicago. He bought the mansion, and his dream was within reach. He had the mansion disassembled. Then carefully marked and numbered each stone component, carefully packed them, and loaded them onto a cargo vessel. The voyage across the great lake was uneventful. The crew dropped anchor and began the task of unloading the large heavy stones, and moving each one onto shore, and up the dunes to the building site. As luck would have it, Mother Nature chose this moment to throw a tantrum. A massive storm blew in, swamping the transport craft, and much of the cargo ended up in Lake Michigan. Some parts of the mansion had been unloaded, but much of it was lost. You can still find a large number of the mansion parts scattered across the top of the dunes on the ***Lost Mansion Trail*** at North Point.

The North Point *"Lost Mansion"* Trail is located in North Point Park south of South Haven, Michigan. The Park is commonly known as the "Old Boy Scout Camp", as this area has been used and maintained by Boy Scouts from Southwest Michigan for many generations. They have had several Eagle Scout Projects in the park, including planting of hundreds of indigenous trees, maintaining the trails, and erosion control measures. The trail head is right next to the road where there is a small parking area. This is a natural trail through a forest of tall trees. Stay on the main trail. After some mild climbing, as the trail wanders upward into the dunes, you will come to a dead end, where you can go right toward the lake or left into more forest. Go left and take the short trail down to another T. Here you go right, and after a short walk will have another gentle climb to the ***mansion ruins.*** Look around carefully and you will find building stones and concrete pillars with their part numbers still visible. As a bonus there is a fantastic view of Lake Michigan. When you are ready to return, you can retrace your route or take a different path. From the ruins return to the T, instead of going left to retrace your path, you can go straight. This will wind through the forest and eventually bring you back to the main trail, where you turn right to the parking area.

North Point Park contains dunes made of sand deposited in the Great Lakes Basin, as the glaciers receded, thousands of years ago. North Point is part of the world's largest freshwater dune system, which stretches 100 miles along this part of Lake Michigan. These coastal sand dunes are special environments that support more unique species of plants, insects, and animals, than any other ecosystem in the Great Lakes Basin.

Local Treasures:

South Haven, Michigan is a very busy place during the tourism season. There are some local treasures that are easy to miss, in all of the hustle and bustle.

Pilgrim Haven & Sea Glass - Pilgrim Haven Natural Area, is a great place if you want to get close to Lake Michigan, without climbing any dunes. The haven is 27 acres, including a stretch of Dyckman Creek, and over 750 linear feet of beach, along Lake Michigan. The property which was used as a camp for over 70 years, is now being protected from development, as a natural area. There is a very easy pathway through the preserve, which includes a picturesque bridge over the creek. The beach is close by, and is covered with stones and pebbles, making it a place where fossils are everywhere and sea glass is being formed constantly. Better parking and barrier-free beach access are planned for the future.

Captain Nemo's, may not be the most famous eating establishment in town, but it is a local favorite for reasonable prices and great food. This is also the place to get that fantastic *Sherman's Ice Cream.*

Visitors to southwest Michigan soon realize that this is blueberry country. *DeGrandchamp Blueberry Farms,* is regularly voted the best U-Pick farm for blueberries. You don't even have to pick them if you don't want to. They have blueberries, ready to go.

Directions:

North Point Park - From downtown South Haven take the Blue Star Highway south. Continue past Route 43 to Ruggles Road to the right. You will only go a short distance, just past 77th St. and there is a small parking area on the right. See the green sign that says North Point Trail.

Pilgrim's Haven - Take the above mentioned 77th St. toward Lake Michigan. Take 18th Ave. west. It should be the first turn west, it is a dead end, there may not be a sign. At the end of that road is Pilgrim's Haven. If you miss 18th Ave. there is another pedestrian access on Fire Lane L.

Important Notes:

North Point Park contains several unmarked trails that branch off the main pathway. If you stay for the sunsets and plan to return to the parking area later, these trails, again unmarked, can be confusing in the dark.

At this writing, 2016, there are no comfort facilities at either trail.

Manton Pathway and Gardens

Manton, Michigan is known in the north as the land of forests and fun. The forests are home to wildlife, scenic trails and the incomparable Manistee River. One of the nature areas that are an integral part of the fun in Manton, is the *Manton Pathway and Gardens* nature walk. As with many of the other treasures and attractions here, you hardly have to leave town to be out enjoying the natural beauty that abounds. The entrance to the Pathway and Gardens is only one city block from the ice cream shop.

The Manton Pathway and Gardens is a 1-1/2 mile nature walk, part of which follows the course of the Manton Creek. The removal of a dam returned the river to its original channel. There is a pond along the stream and a picturesque walking bridge now crosses the stream, at the site of the old dam. This is an easy walk with stops and benches staggered along the trails. The presence of the stream and pond ensure that you will see a wide range of Michigan birds, in every season. Another feature that makes this trail so much fun is the number of grassy areas that have been groomed, making it easy to find a picnic spot. The Manton Pathways location has also become a destination for the geo-cache crowd. There is one cache here, hidden away off the trail. Again, the in town location of this trail makes it a favorite for those who may not be able to handle more remote wilderness areas.

Manton is a great site for all kinds of trails. It is not an exaggeration to say that you can snowmobile and ski right outside your back door. Snowmobile trails crisscross Wexford County throughout the City of Manton.

Local Treasures:

The *Veteran's Memorial Museum,* in Manton, has among its exhibits a footlocker from the *Revolutionary War*.   Constructed and dedicated in 2002, the museum was entirely achieved by donations of material and labor. The Museum is owned by the City of Manton, and the Museum Board. It is run and managed by volunteers. The Veteran's Memorial Museum Project was recognized as #1 in the nation by the Veteran's of Foreign Wars.

The Manistee River is just north of Manton, Michigan, and provides some of the most pristine river scenes and experiences anywhere in Michigan. The *Horseshoe Bend,* is a favorite destination on the river. This part of the river is a perfect choice for floating and kayaking. The river and trails wind through pines, hardwoods, wetlands and valleys. Every kind of Northern Michigan wildlife can be found here. When you get down to the dam, you can pause and watch the eagles fly. A float trip will also bring you to two unique bridges: an arch timber bridge, crossing Slagle Creek and a suspension bridge over the Manistee River, linking the north end of the trail with the Marilla segment of the North Country Trail, on the west side of the river.

A Bit of History:

The Wexford County seat was moved to Manton in the 1880's, in an attempt to resolve a feud between citizens of Sherman and Cadillac.

Cadillac managed to win the county seat by a county-wide vote in 1882. The next day a posse led by the sheriff, made their way to Manton intending to collect the county records. They hadn't quite finished the job when an angry crowd gathered and ran them out of town. Thus ended the first skirmish in the *Battle of Manton*. It wasn't quite over.

The sheriff and his bunch returned to Cadillac to regroup. Folks in Manton styled it as more of a retreat. The sheriff gathered a force of several hundred armed men. Some say the force was further reinforced by a brass band. This group, some of whom may have been imbibing, traveled back to Manton, to finish seizing the records. The residents of Manton resisted and even barricaded the courthouse, but to no avail. The Cadillac marauders got all the documents and returned in triumph to Cadillac. Thus ended, the Battle of Manton.

Directions:

Manton Pathway and Gardens, is open year round Monday - Sunday 8:00 a.m. to 8:00 p.m. The trail head is located about a ¼ mile north of the main intersection in town. Turn west on Cedar St. next to the Dairy Bar.

Important Notes:

The pathways are gravel, grass, and wood chips. Manton is about 10 miles north of Cadillac.

Moccasin Flower Trail

In a small stand of woods, in Rycenga Park, is a system of trails. These are beautiful nature trails, plunked down in a rather busy urban area between Muskegon and Grand Rapids. One loop is known locally as the *Moccasin Flower Trail*. Much of the park has been developed by the school system so it includes sports fields, playgrounds, picnic areas, and restroom facilities. The nature trails are away from all the activity, so you can enjoy the quiet of a forest walk. There is a separate parking area right at the trail entrance.

From the parking area there are three options for entering the trail system. All of them loop back, so you have several choices as to the distance of the walk. The right hand trail follows the outside border of the system, taking you through the towering oaks, with pine trees scattered within. After a medium length walk, you come to an observation deck, overlooking a wetland. Keeping to this trail will take hikers all the way around the nature area, along the *Moccasin Flower Trail*, and back to the parking area. The center trail goes almost directly to the observation deck. About half way along the center trail is a branch going to the left, that leads directly to the Moccasin Flower Trail.

The Moccasin Flower, or, as it is commonly known, the Lady's Slipper, blooms in the spring in a great profusion of colors. This flower also likes streams and wet areas. The section of the Rycenga nature trails, where these flowers bloom, has been improved with an excellent boardwalk that follows the course of the stream. Hikers of all skill levels will find it easy to view the blooms growing along the stream, without getting wet and muddy. There are twists and turns to the boardwalk so you get to view the area from several angles. It is wide enough so you can pause, without blocking others. Eventually you reach another cross trail. Going right, will lead to another observation deck and then back to the parking area. Going left, is the short way back to the parking area.

This entire trail system is sheltered by old trees, so this walk is almost always in the shade, making it a cool, refreshing pause even on very warm days. It is easy to forget that there are housing developments all around. The name, "Moccasin Flower Trail", isn't used much anymore. Even the locals have forgotten the old designation. Some think the flower was so named by early settlers because of its shape, before the wildflower became known as the Lady's Slipper. With all of the improvements to the park, you could spend all day here.

Local Treasures:

Only about 15 minutes from the trails, in Allendale, is the ***Engine House No. 5 Museum***, one of the most unusual in Michigan. Built in 1880, it isn't just the beautiful historic architecture, nor is it the remarkable and rare artifacts inside. Unlike so many historic buildings lost to the wrecking ball, this one was saved from demolition at the last minute. Preventing demolition was only the beginning, the building had to be moved. The engine house site, Leonard and Monroe streets in Grand Rapids, was needed for a new modern fire station. The building was dismantled brick by brick, and the whole works was put into storage. They did it in 10 weeks and 2 days. In 1985 reassembly began and the museum opened to the public in 1986. Just learning the full story of the problems that had to be solved makes a trip to the museum worth it.

Inside on the polished wood floor, are displays of fire equipment, and memorabilia, some of which is extremely rare. This is an historic firehouse, so it has two levels connected by a stairway going up, and a fire pole going down through a hole in the floor, that the firemen used when they responded to an alarm. It is worth going upstairs just to see the gorgeous chandelier in the break room, another treasure, that was literally pulled out of the trash heap. There are fire trucks, steam pumpers, and even a fire truck that was hauled to the site of the fire, by men instead of horses. The collection of equipment and memorabilia is extensive, so plan for some time. The tour is well done and informative. There are treasures and rare items all through the museum. One item that fascinates young people, is the fire box switching machine. It made emergency response possible in the days before WiFi and telephones in every pocket. This is a complex machine that went into action when a fire alarm box was activated, somewhere in the city. It would calculate the location of the fire, so the firemen knew where to go. It is an amazing machine and often baffles a generation, who have never been without a digital connection to the world around them.

Great Train Robbery – If you've ever dreamed of riding the rails the old fashion way or even witnessing train robbers at work, Coopersville, Michigan, is the place for you. The Coopersville & Marne Railway is an all-volunteer historic railway operating vintage locomotives and circa-1920's cars. They run about seven miles from Coopersville, Mich. to Marne, from spring to winter in all weathers. They have several special events through the season including The Great Train Robbery.

This historic stretch of track is right where it has been since the 1850's. Preserving this right-of-way requires replacing worn parts which is often done just as it was back in the day, by hand. They have a number of special events throughout the year.

Just minutes away from Rycenga Park, is one of the best shops in the state if you are looking for products that are made in Michigan. At *Maggie's Gourmet Foods & Gifts* you will find a wide selection of gift baskets, gourmet foods and specialty products. Each of their products and gift baskets is specially designed to convey a message of generosity and caring. Maggie's is known for one of the largest selection of Michigan made products under one roof.

Directions:

Rycenga Park, is on the outskirts of Fruitport. Fruitport is east of Muskegon off Interstate 96 on E. Fruitport Road. Go west toward Fruitport, turn north on 3rd Ave. Turn west at the light on to W. Fruitport Road. The entrance to Rycenga Park, 16255 W. Fruitport Road, is a couple of miles at the junction with W. Springlake Road on the right. The trail head is to the left away from all the athletics fields.

Engine House No. 5 Museum – Take the 68th St. Exit south off I-96 toward Eastmanville. Go south until you reach Route 45, then go east toward Allendale. Engine House No. 5 is on the south side of Route 45.

Important Notes:

The gates at ***Rycenga Park*** are locked at dusk!!

Engine House No. 5, is open afternoons Wednesday through Saturday, check their website for updates.

THE

NAHMA

GENERAL STORE

WAS

FEATURED

ON

AMERICAN

PICKERS

Nahma Marsh Trail

The tiny community of Nahma, in the upper peninsula of Michigan, is home to the *Nahma Marsh Trail*, a place where dark skies delight star-gazers, the Milky Way is easy to photograph, and the Aurora Borealis displays fantastic colorful curtains of light. This linear trail once crept under a dense cedar forest, but a windstorm in 1997 leveled the trees leaving hikers today with broad vistas of the marsh. The walk is fairly level, with benches every 200 feet or so along the way, leading to the main viewing area. It is only 0.3 mile walk, on the fully accessible hard-surfaced trail, through the wet conifer forest which contains tamarack, balsam fir, black spruce and white cedar trees, to the two-tiered viewing platform. In addition to bald eagles and ospreys, bird watchers may also see species such as the yellow-bellied flycatcher, golden-crowned kinglet, white-throated sparrow, red-breasted nuthatch, Nashville warbler, black-and-white warbler, American goldfinch and cedar waxwing.

You can make a day of it in the forests here, by taking a leisurely float down the *Sturgeon River*. From the highway, US 2, the river meanders through the Hiawatha National Forest. The whole float is only a few miles ending near Nahma, at Lake Michigan. This is an unimproved stretch of river, that is cleared each spring. It hasn't been discovered by most paddlers yet, so there is no commercialization to interfere with a pure forest experience. Bald eagles commonly nest along the river, especially near the Nahma Marsh Trailhead. Kayaks are available in Nahma.

Local Treasures:

For decades there were reports of strange twisting clouds, high above Lake Michigan south of **Stonington Point**. The reports were generally dismissed as having no validity. Then the age of digital cameras and hand-held video arrived. It was discovered that the unusual clouds were real, and that they were actually enormous flocks of Monarch butterflies. Every autumn, during the last two weeks of August and the first two weeks of September, the Monarchs gather near the old, abandoned lighthouse. There they wait until the winds are right for the migration flight, south across Lake Michigan, Green Bay, and on to their winter grounds in Mexico.

Probably the most famous attraction in this area is **Fayette**. Fayette is a restored historic town, which was once one of the most productive iron-smelting operations in the Upper Peninsula. There were huge furnaces, an extensive dock, and several kilns in operation at the settlement. Nearly 500 people lived and worked there for 20+ years, in a town that existed just to produce pig iron. Today, the site is well maintained and restored. The grounds are an easy walk, and the surrounding scenery is really breathtaking. You can get an excellent orientation and overview of this area, by visiting the welcome center. They have a model of the entire site and thorough historical documentation.

A full day exploring these three peninsulas will require a proper breakfast. Just head over to **Jacks** in downtown Rapid River. They open early, have cinnamon rolls the size of dinner plates, and this is the only place I know, where you can get Yooper Eggs Benedict.

You can get all the information you need about the region, good food, and comfortable lodgings at the historic *Nahma Inn*. The hotel was built in 1909 for employees of the Bay De Noc Lumber Company. Nahma, was designed and built as a company town, complete with a grand boulevard with a grassy medium. The Inn is thought to be graced by the spirit of a lady who once resided and worked in the kitchen. The helpful spirit is known to organize things in the kitchen and rearrange objects when nobody is around!

A Bit of History:

"NAHMA", which is an Indian word meaning sturgeon, was established in 1881 by the Bay De Noquet Lumber Company of Oconto, Wisconsin. A stop in Nahma, is an opportunity to step back in time, and get an idea of what a "Company town" was like in the late 1800's and the early 1900's. The Bay De Noquet Lumber Company headquartered in Nahma, as the base for its operation Michigan's Upper Peninsula. The company had a 70 year life span in from 1881, until it cut and processed it's last log on July 26, 1951. The Bay De Noquet Lumber Company, processed over 2,500,000,000 board feet of lumber in Nahma.

Directions:

The GG Road, Route 497, is the paved road that goes from US 2 to Nahma along the course of the Sturgeon River. The parking area for the Nahma Marsh Trail is on this road.

The road to Stonington Point is just east of Rapid River. Fayette is to the east, on the Garden Peninsula.

Important Notes:

The Nahma Marsh Trail is not maintained in winter, bring snowshoes. The parking area for the trail is gravel.

The last mile of the 17 mile drive to Stonington Point is gravel. There is a parking area before the last mile, hikers can walk in from there.

Northport Trails

The last community going north, up the Leelanau Peninsula, is Northport, Michigan. The road continues north to the tip of the peninsula, and along the way is the trail to **Cathead Bay,** leading to the **Manitou Overlook**. The trail is part of a system located in a new section of Leelanau State Park, at the end of Densmore Road. There are several trails that begin at the parking area, all of them are very well marked. For the Cathead Bay, follow Spur 1. The trail is fairly smooth through gently rolling terrain. The area is forested with tall beech, white birch, and pines, with a scattering of other hardwoods. There are a couple of small hills to negotiate, as the trail winds through the forest. This trail follows the contours of the landscape, affording great views of several ravines. At each juncture with other trail spurs, is an excellent map sign, showing the options. The spurs to the overlook are well marked. After less than a mile, you reach the **stairs to the overlook**. The stairway is only about 30 steps, but it is there, and it is steep. At the top is an overlook, rewarding the climb with an unequaled view of the dunes, and the Manitou Islands in the distance. Plan ahead for sunset watching, this is a popular spot for that.

If the stairs are too much for you, there is another unique **flat shoreline trail,** nearby. Drive further north to the tip of the peninsula and enter the State Park. From the parking area, it is just a short walk out to the **Grand Traverse Lighthouse.** There is a pathway that goes out to the shoreline, past the old Fog Signal Building, and winds back to the grounds of the lighthouse. The trail is narrow and is made mostly of stone, but it is smooth and easy to walk. The trail winds along the shore of Lake Michigan, through stands of Pussy Willows, low shrubs, and small trees. The entire walk is only about a quarter mile, but there are gorgeous views of the distant islands, and the lake. The variety of birds found here is amazing. If you are early, the benches make this a comfortable spot to watch the sunrise.

Perhaps the least known trail in the area, is the *Nagonaba Nature Trail,* found right in Northport. Beginning in town, the 3/4-mile trail curves through some unique habitats, and ends at Morningside Drive, near the Braman Hill Recreation Area. The trail was designed to give access to three areas, each with different natural characteristics. The first part goes through larch, tamarack, and pine trees with a small bridge across the Northport Creek. It is in this section where everyone stops for a selfie with a big cool sculpture, *Jeremy the Frog*, the work of a local artist. In the spring season this area will be covered in marsh marigolds, and jack-in-the-pulpit peaking up through the wetlands. The next two areas include a section of cedars, hemlocks, and quaking aspen trees. Then comes a section of hardwoods including ash, beech, and maple. There are small signs along the way, to help with tree identification, and boardwalks protect the low wet areas. A spur leads to a wooded ridge. The sign says it is steep, and that one should be sure-footed. That is an understatement.

Local Treasures:

The Historic *Willowbrook Mill*, (circa 1850), sponsored this chapter, and is a favorite stop for day trippers to Northport. This charming spot has a registered trout stream, Northport Creek, running directly under the building, and features a water wheel. This is the only building in the State of Michigan constructed over a trout stream. You may even see salmon swimming upstream in spawning season. The patio, at the waterwheel, is a great spot to relax, enjoy the running water, and take a few pictures. These folks are well known for their gelato, and for the gift shop featuring the work of Michigan artisans.

Just across the street from the mill, is Barb's Bakery. Whatever you do, don't leave town without trying her *Cinnamon Twist*. I have never had anything like it. You may as well buy at least two of them while you are there. Otherwise, you will have to go back, because one is only going to make your mouth water for another one.

The beach at the trail network, where the Manitou Overlook is found, is narrow sand and rock along several low dune ridges. These open dunes, with clear blowouts, protect sand and gravel flats that are nesting areas for state-endangered *piping plovers*. This is an unusual spot to find these birds nesting, and the open spaces make photographing them easier. At some times during May, June, and July, parts of the dunes will be closed, so as not to disturb the plovers on their nests.

The tip of the Leelanau Peninsula is marked by the *Grand Traverse Lighthouse*, one of the oldest on the Great Lakes. This lighthouse guided ships through the Manitou Passage of Lake Michigan, for nearly 150 years. The lighthouse has a museum representing a keeper's home, and several other exhibits. The old fog horn station is also on the grounds, and is used for demonstrations.

A Bit of History:

Northport Creek, a designated trout stream, was known as Big Sucker Creek back in the day. The Nagonaba Trail was named for one of three Native Americans who accompanied the Rev. George N. Smith when he moved to the Leelanau Peninsula from Allegan County. The name may have been spelled "Nagonabe".

Directions:

The Cathead Bay Trail access is on Densmore Road, just north of the Woolsey Memorial Airport, on the way to the lighthouse.

The Grand Traverse Lighthouse is at the tip of the Leelanau Peninsula. From Northport, get on Route 201, and go north to the lighthouse and park. The road is called County 629 as well.

The in town access, to Nagonaba Trail, is at the west end of Nagonaba Street about 4 blocks from downtown Northport.

Important Notes:

The parking area to Cat Head Bay is gravel.

The Nagonaba is a natural trail. Expect some marshy ground and mud in the spring.

THERE

ARE

SEVERAL

DARK SKY

PARKS

IN

MICHIGAN

Old Growth Red Pines Trail

This trail winds its way through the ***Red Pines Natural Area.*** The pathway threads its way through fairly flat terrain, in a natural area, that has not been altered by the hand of man, since European explorers rediscovered it. At one time, this grove of old-growth red pines and jack pines, was home to the largest red pine in Michigan, a former National Champion red pine. That old champion pine is no longer living, but there are several gigantic members of the species, still standing in this forest.

The trail is about 1 ½ miles long. There is a wonderful variety of plant life and tree species, in addition to the towering red pines. At more than a dozen spots on the trail, the DNR has installed interpretive signs and benches. The signs greatly enhance the experience for novices and experienced hikers alike. The information provided makes it possible to understand the forest as a living thing, with a history and a future. The walk is silent, due to the pine needles covering the ground; each step on this walking trail releases more of the pine scent, that fills the air.

This 34-acre grove of virgin red pine is one of the best stands left in the mid-west portion of the United States. It is an excellent example of the virgin pine forest, that once covered this part of Michigan. As you walk through the stand, there are points where you are completely surrounded by giant trees. When you reach the center point of the grove, it is easy to imagine that you have traveled to the past, back to the time when the great forests covered all of Northern Michigan. There is evidence of the great fires that swept through in 1798, 1888, and 1928, yet the towering pines remain.

Local Treasures:

Fireman's Memorial - Standing twelve feet tall, and weighing around 2,000 pounds, the bronze firefighter symbolizes the very best of us. The statue at the *Fireman's Memorial* was created by Michigan craftsman Edward Chesney. This memorial is dedicated to the members of that unselfish organization, of men and women, who hold devotion to duty above personal risk, who count sincerity of service above personal comfort and convenience, and who strive unceasingly, to find better ways of protecting the lives, homes, and property of their fellow citizens, from the ravages of fire and other disasters. Each year, usually on the 3rd weekend in September, the Michigan Firemen's Memorial Festival, takes place over three days. The grounds include picnic and play areas.

Directions:

The *Red Pines* trail head is 8 miles N of St. Helen or 7 miles south of M-18 on Sunset Rood via F-97 or from CR-602 near Kirtland College. After turning off F-97, the half mile road to the parking area is gravel.

The *Firemen's Memorial* is just south of Roscommon about 1/2 mile east of M-18.

Important Notes:

The parking area and approach to the Red Pines Natural Area is gravel. The sign says, hiking time is one half hour.

BORTELL'S

NORTH

OF

PENTWATER

IS

FAMOUS

FOR

SMOKED

FISH

Pentwater Pathways

South of Pentwater Lake, in the middle of a major Michigan tourism area, is a nearly pristine network of paths and trails known as the ***Pentwater Pathways***. The Pentwater Pathways are gorgeous for a summer hike. The trails cover mostly soft rolling hills, are heavily wooded and offer abundant wildlife. There are 7.2 different trail miles here within the Pere' Marquette State Forest, under the care of the Michigan Department of Natural Resources.

These trails were originally designed and built for cross country ski use and are groomed in the winter. Word spread and the snowshoe crowd began to show up, then the mountain bikers found the pathways. The trail system includes four different loops, totaling 15 miles. From a skiing point of view, there are beginner to advanced trails. These days the trails and pathways are mostly used for walking in the warm months. They are too gentle and easy to attract the extreme mountain bikers.

Being close to the major north – south highway, the pathways make a nice place to take a break. There are dense woodlands, wildflowers, and abundant wildlife. No motorized vehicles are allowed, making this a quiet place.

Local Treasures:

Most visitors to this area flock to the dunes, beaches and lighthouses, but there are some hidden treasures nearby. Silver Lake is a focal point and a visit to **SunChasers Souvenirs** will pay off. These folks helped make this chapter possible. If you are looking for quality made in Michigan gifts, this is the place to go. They have the souvenirs, ORV flags, and all the local knowledge you need to find the local treasures that are often overlooked in this part of Oceana County, known as Little Point Sable.

The **Lavender Labyrinth**, would be an outstanding attraction anywhere. It is a labyrinth made of live blooming lavender that covers several acres. The labyrinth is on the grounds of Cherry Point Farm west of Shelby and is a perfect place to walk amid lavender, rocks and wildflowers. There is no charge, and reservations are not needed. Even if you don't have time for a stroll, it is worth taking a look just to enjoy the sheer beauty of the labyrinth. The site is open to everyone and is in full bloom in July and August.

There are two other noteworthy stops near the labyrinth. Just to the west on Buchanan Road, is the **Old Stone Church**. Constructed of field stone, this church makes a cool backdrop for vacation or getaway photos.

Go east on Buchanan Road to 18th Ave. and then north about a mile to the **Fox Barn Winery**. For generations they have cared for 2,000 acres, much of which is planted with fruit trees. The tasting room is a unique setting inside the restored antique barn. Wine tasting and snacks can be enjoyed at the bar, or under an umbrella on the outdoor patio.

A family favorite in this area is the ***Lewis Farm Market and Petting Zoo***, in New Era. One of their older orchards has been re-purposed into barnyards to house a sensational collection of unusual animals and birds. Great fun for kids of all ages.

A really fun way to cool off from all this hiking and walking, is to go tubing down ***Stony Creek.*** Stony Creek Lake is just a few miles from Silver Lake. Tubes are available right there, and the float is only about an hour. The stream is gentle, and not too deep. The excursion is especially suited for families, and ends right at Oval Beach on Lake Michigan.

A one of a kind treasure is the exhibit of ***Animated Dolls***, in the Hart Historic District, guaranteed to amaze and delight boys and girls of all ages. The displays depict scenes from daily life from the pioneer era, from playing a piano, to churning butter, to feeding the baby. All of this comes to life when the power is turned on and the fabulous animated dolls and puppets go into action. The scenes and animation are so cool that smiles breakout and everyone begins to clap. These fantastic dolls were originally used in displays at the, now closed, Powers Department Store in Hart. There just isn't another display like this anywhere in Michigan.

Directions:

To find the ***Pentwater Pathways***, take the Pentwater Monroe Road exit off US-31, turn west on Long Bridge Road, go across thc bridge, and then south on Wayne Road. The entrance is about one mile south.

From the pathways, go back to Long Bridge Road and head toward Lake Michigan to Ridge Road which will take you to Silver Lake and ***SunChasers Souvenirs.*** From there you can take North 18th Ave south to W. Buchanan Road go east to Cherry Point Farm and the ***Lavender Labyrinth***.

The ***Animated Dolls***, are in the Hart Historic District, near downtown Hart.

Important Notes:

When you leave the main road at the Pentwater Pathways entrance, you will be on a short drive, that is gravel. The parking area is a widened space in the road, 0.3 mile in, and you will notice the bench, at the entrance to the trail system on your right.

The Hart Historic District is open weekends.

Petroglyph Trail

This trail is located at the site of the ***Sanilac Petroglyphs***. The petroglyphs are the only verified sandstone glyph carvings in Michigan. Enigmatic, sometimes bizarre, images are carved into nearly an acre of sandstone out in the forest in Sanilac County. From the parking area, there is a groomed trail that leads into the forest, with interpretive signs and side trails along the way. At the site of the petroglyphs, the main hiking trail branches off. Some of the small side trails are worth exploring. One of them leads to a grove of giant maple trees.

The main trail is one loop of about a mile. It winds through the forest and crosses the Cass River, via small suspension bridges, in two places. The trail is narrow in places and can be rough due to tree roots growing near the surface. The topography is quite varied. The forest and undergrowth are very dense where the trail crosses the river or passes near wetlands. In a couple of places, beaver activity has dammed the river forming small ponds. Then there are the huge rock formations. Giant slabs of rock are visible along the way. Many of these were underwater at one time, back when the Cass River was nearly a mile wide. Another unique feature of this trail is the towering White Pine growing just off the trail. This tree is estimated to be over 125 years old. It probably sprouted right after the the last of the great firestorms in 1881. Those firestorms and the winds that followed helped expose the petroglyphs.

Further on the trail winds through a more open area.

There is evidence of an old logging camp near one clearing and even some old fruit trees. The hike passes near a large rock. It was at this point that the Old Cass Road crossed the river. All that is left are remnants of the old abutments and a two track leading to the river. This part of the trail is in an area that is quite open. A variety of wildlife can be seen here along with a great variety of mushrooms. The trail goes back into the hardwood forest and descends down to the river and the second suspension bridge. After crossing the river, the trail turns to the east and back to the petroglyphs. Interpretive signs enhance the experience all along the trail. The trail is open all year.

The Treasure:

There are hundreds of pictures carved into a large sandstone outcropping. Some of the more unusual images, like the 6 finger hand and the man with the conical hat, still offer puzzles to be solved. There are carvings that are readily understood like the coyote, rabbit. and bird tracks. There are spirals like those found in carvings all over the world. Then there are the carvings that seem to be representations of fantastic animals or even, as some say, unusual letters and scripts. The trail of coyote tracks that cross the sandstone are part of the carvings and run almost perfectly south to north.

Some of the glyphs are difficult to interpret, like the man with the conical hat equipped with bow and arrow. There are hands with 4 or 6 fingers, unidentified animals, and symbolic shapes. There are several interpretations of the meaning and origins of the carvings. The rock outcropping is protected by a fence and a roof. During the summer season volunteers are on hand to allow visitors to get up close to the carvings. They also offer an entertaining and educational program describing the carvings. This program is the best way to get accurate information about the interpretations of the glyphs.

The discovery of these unique carvings was a happy result of the horrendous firestorms that swept through the "thumb" region at the end of the lumbering era. In 1871, farmers were using fires to clear their land. Those fires got out of control destroying 2 million acres of forest and killing 200 people. In 1881, another fire swept across the thumb. This fire burned a million acres in one day and killed 282 people. The fires and heat were so intense that railroad rails were twisted and entire towns were obliterated. After the fire, strong west winds blew through, the topsoil was swept away revealing the long hidden carvings.

Directions:

From Highway 25 on the Lake Huron shore, take Bay City-Forestville Rd. west to Germania Rd. Go south about 1/2 mile and you will reach the park where these remarkable carvings are located.

PIERS

GORGE

CONTAINS

SEVERAL

CATARACTS

ON

THE

MENOMINEE

RIVER

Piers Gorge Trail

Near Iron Mountain, in the southwestern upper peninsula, the Menominee River defines the Michigan – Wisconsin border, and flows through the forests and hills to empty into Green Bay and Lake Michigan. This part of Michigan is often described as picturesque, due to the scenic overlooks, waterfalls, and color tours. One of the most beautiful places on the entire Menominee River is the *Trail at Piers Gorge*. Only a few miles south of Norway, Michigan, the river rips through this gorge producing a spectacular show, that is easily accessible to nearly anyone. What is more, this is a spot to return to in every season. It is just as inviting, as a winter walk, as it is in the warmth of summer.

A few miles south of Norway, is a large sign announcing the road to Piers Gorge. A short drive on that road brings you to a small gravel parking area. The pathway leads into the silent trees, and takes you to the gentle trail, that follows the course of the river. The *Piers Gorge Trail* was first used by Native Americans to portage around the falls, that plunge and roar through the gorge. After just a few minutes of walking, the only sound you will hear will be the falling waters in the distance.

The pathway is not improved, but is quite smooth, and easy to follow. As you walk, you are moving upstream, and will reach the first cataract in only a few minutes. The walk along the river brings you to different viewing spots, sometimes above a white-water rapids. When you reach the third cataract, you will be rewarded with a magnificent view of a wild roaring waterfall, in the distance. There are four different falls or rapids along the pathway. It is easy to forget, that you are only about 8 miles from town, instead of in the middle of some vast unexplored wilderness.

Local Treasures:

Just up the hill off main street in Iron Mountain, Michigan, is one of the wonders of the mechanical and steam age. Inside the Cornish Pumping Engine & Mining Museum, is the *Cornish Pumping Engine*. The Chapin Mine, which opened in the late 1870's, was one of the wettest mines in history. Eventually, to handle the water flowing into the mine shafts, they had to adapt technology previously only used in the deep tin mines of Cornwall.

The Cornish Pump is simply overwhelming when you first see it. The flywheel is 40 feet in diameter and requires a slot in the floor that is 20 feet deep, to accommodate it. The shaft for that flywheel is 24 inches in diameter and the pump itself is 54 feet tall. The piston stroke is 10 feet and produced just 10 revolutions per minute, on the flywheel. This engine weighs in at over 700 tons. It was able to drive a series of pumps that lifted water from 1,500 feet deep in the earth. The whole rig could move 3,000 gallons of water out of the mines every minute. 5,000,000 gallons could be removed from the mines every day.

Across the street, from the building housing the pump engine, is another building where artisans are restoring/replicating one of the famous *CG4A WWII Gliders*. These gliders carried troops across the English Channel during the D Day Invasion of World War II. There are only a couple of these aircraft in Michigan.

Also within a few miles of Piers Gorge is the *Rainbow's End Alpaca Farm*. Rainbow Gifts & Yarn is a place, "where shopping becomes an experience!" In their 1,700 square foot store you will find beautiful alpaca apparel such as sweaters, coats, scarves, hats, mittens, and their ever popular socks. On the other side of the store, the fiber enthusiast will find many types of quality yarn, needles, notions and patterns. A virtual fiber haven, the farm is well known for the Rainbow Gold Yarn produced by Rainbow's End Alpacas.

Directions:

The road to the gorge is south of Norway, Michigan on Route 8. Norway is just a few miles east of Iron Mountain.

Important Notes:

Part of the road to the parking area at Piers Gorge is gravel. The gorge and the pathway are in a wilderness area; there are no facilities here.

The Mining Museum is open during the summer months.

THE

HEMINGWAY

COTTAGE

WINDEMERE

IS

ON

WALLOON

LAKE

Postle Farm Preserve Trails

Northwest Michigan has become a famous for its resorts and tourist destinations. The fame has brought explosive growth, urban development, and crowds. Right in the middle of it all is the ***Postle Farm Preserve***. In a region where most nature preserves are kind of wild, this one preserves an historic agricultural environment. The Postle Farm Preserve consists of 113 acres, encompassing three distinct habitats. The habitats include, an open field farmstead area, a northern hardwood forest area and a low meadow wetland area. Each habitat can be explored via easy loop trails in a family friendly environment. The longest loop is only one mile long.

The trails are well marked to guide hikers through the various regions, each with its unique character and wildlife. There are a few interpretive stations along the way. Upon leaving the parking area, the entry path leads to one of the original barns, now used as a visitor center. There are exhibits inside, open in season, and period farm equipment is on display outside. The entry trail continues for a short distance to a signpost, where you can choose the Open Fields and Farmstead habitat or take a branch that leads into the Northern Hardwood Forest habitat.

The trail through the hardwood habitat slopes gently downhill into the woods consisting of beech, maple, evergreen and hemlock trees. About a third of the way along the trail, a second loop, marked in red, is an option for a longer hike. Continuing on, the original loop will take you to the third habitat, the Wetland and Lower Meadow. A trail follows the course of a small stream, for a short distance, before turning back in the direction of the farmstead area. After a short walk, you arrive at a spur that leads to a region the preserve has named, the Hemlock Cathedral. At the end of the spur, you find yourself in a grove of towering hemlock trees.

The Postle Farm Preserve contains some of the first cross country ski trails ever developed in Northern Michigan. Long before the sport became a craze, these trails were created by a few enthusiasts from the Sierra Club. While many of the natural areas near Petoskey have been lost to development, and others are crowded much of the year, the Postle Farm Preserve, in the heart of it all, is a place where families can go to wander the quiet meadows and forests of an historic farmstead, right in the middle of all the hustle and bustle.

Local Treasures:

After a pleasant nature break at the Preserve, the Walloon Lake district, is a favorite spot for refreshment and shopping. The *Vintage Mercantile,* an antique and home decor shop, sponsors this chapter, and attracts treasure seekers from all over the region. Vintage Mercantile is located directly across the street from Hotel Walloon. Many of their items are unique to Northern Michigan, especially Walloon Lake's, historic past. The store has been nominated for best Antique and Vintage store in the Petoskey News Best of 2016 competition! The shop is located in an historic cabin and is filled top to bottom with antiques and vintage finds. Plan to spend some time inside, the variety of merchandise is amazing, and there is no space that isn't filled to capacity.

Shopping and hiking can build an appetite. If you want to sit by the lake and have an eclectic dining adventure, the menu at the Barrel Back is for you. If you are looking for simpler fare that is wholesome and delicious, the deli at the Walloon Lake General Store is the place to go.

A Bit of History:

This is Ernest Hemingway country. There is an historical marker across from Walloon Lake that tells some of the story. Today, you can still walk the trails that Hemingway walked, and see the sites he saw. The cottage of Windemere is still there at Walloon Lake, though it is not open to the public. This region inspired two books, "Up in Michigan" and "Big Two-Hearted River".

Directions:

Walloon Lake is off Highway 131, halfway between Boyne Falls and Petoskey. Just north of the road to Walloon Lake is Country Club Road. Go west on Country Club Road for about one mile. The *Postle Farm Preserve* entrance is just after a 90 degree turn and is marked by a large wooden sign.

Important Notes:

The preserve lies within the Walloon Lake Watershed and is under the protection of the Walloon Lake Trust and Conservancy. It is one of the largest tracts preserved by the Conservancy. The last half mile to the Preserve is a gravel road.

Primeval Forest Trail

This walking trail winds through the only remaining old growth, beech-maple climax forest in lower Michigan. The trail is located in the 311-acre, ***Warren Woods State Park***. The gigantic beech and maple trees that form the forest occupy 200 of those acres, sheltering one of the most beautiful walking trails in southwest Michigan. There are two ways to enter the forest, a small trail head north and the state park entrance south. Regardless of which you choose, there are about 3.5 miles of trails that loop along the Galien River. Near the center of the forest, a fine pedestrian bridge crosses the river connecting the two halves of the woods. The north approach to the bridge descends to the river. On the south side of the bridge, is an interpretive station with information and benches. There are 40 easy shallow steps, down the stairs to the bridge.

Visitors who enter from the State Park entrance on Elm Valley Road, will have a short drive to parking, and minimal facilities. The trail head is right at the parking area, and takes hikers straight into the forest, and some really good places for bird watching.

Those who enter from the north trail head, at Warren Woods Road, will immediately be surrounded by enormous beech and maple trees. The trail winds through the gigantic trees some of which are more than 100 feet tall, with a girth so great you can't get your arms all the way around, when you hug them. A short distance in, you come to a fork in the trail. Going left will take you on a somewhat rough track to the Galien River. The right fork is a gentler trail that also leads to the river right where the foot bridge is located.

No matter which pathway is chosen, one is nearly overwhelmed by the silent beauty of these majestic trees. The unusual wildflowers on the ground, and the variety of birds in the canopy above, complete a nature experience, which is only possible in this last remaining beech-maple climax forest. This fantastic woodland is so little known that, even in the middle of summer, when rangers are turning people away from the dunes park, a few miles away on Lake Michigan, you might be the only hiker breathing the cool pure forest air.

Local Treasures:

Warren Dunes State Park is the place to go, if you want to play on the ***sand dunes***. The dunes rise over 250 feet above the Lake Michigan shoreline. There are almost 2,000 acres here, with miles of hiking trails yet, the park can be very crowded in the summer months. This is also a favorite destination for hang gliders.

Inland from Lake Michigan, is the historic community of Buchanan. A couple of miles north of town is ***Bear Cave***. The cave was formed over 10,000 years ago, as a result of the glacial drift, and is the only cavern in lower Michigan. The glacier receding left behind Tufa and boulders which make up the construction of the cave.

This is not a gigantic cavern, such as those found at Mammoth Cave or the Carlsbad Caverns. Rather this is a small natural cave, with multiple rooms. The whole thing is only about 150 feet.

As you descend down the winding stairs into the cavern, you will see a Kansas Boulder, thought to be tens of thousands of years old. While damp, the way is well lit and the various formations are well marked, making for a very informative experience. Toward the back of the cave is a secondary passage that leads to a low roofed room, with a large clear pool of water. Beyond the low ceiling and pool is another hidden room. This room is known as the "Slave Room" because it was used to hide slaves, making their way to freedom on the "underground railroad".

A Bit of History:

This treasured forest might have been lost forever, if not for the demands of fashion and a shortage of whale bone, for ladies' corsets back in the 1800's. The whales were becoming scarce in the great oceans, due to over harvesting. A critical component necessary to create that feminine curve formed by ladies' corsets, was whalebone. No whalebone for the corsets meant, no curves, and no curves meant a major crisis was upon us. Fortunately for everyone, Mr. Edward K. Warren, discovered a way to substitute turkey-wing feathers for the increasingly scarce whalebone, established the Warren Featherbone Company, saved the day and made a fortune.

Like so many industrialists and robber barons of his day, Mr. Warren dedicated a portion of his wealth to saving the environment. In 1879, only seven years after the country's first national park, Yellowstone, was established, he purchased a stand of virgin timber to save it from the timber industry. That stand of trees would become Warren Woods. In addition, he bought a stretch of Lake Michigan dunes, considered worthless at the time, which are today the popular Warren Dunes State Park.

Directions:

Bear Cave, is located a couple miles north of Buchanan on the Red Bud Trail. There is a small fee to tour Bear Cave and it is only open in season.

The south entrance to ***Warrens Woods***, off W. Elm Valley Road, is the State Park Entrance and is only open after April 1. It takes you onto a gravel drive that leads to the parking area. The north entrance is just a path. North end parking, is simply pulling on to the side of the Warren Woods Rd. There are only a few parking spots, but you can park and walk the trail during the off-season months.

Rainbow Trail

Travelers who discover Drummond Island, often return again and again. The profusion of natural wonders and scenic views, lure one back. Trails on the island tend to be pretty rough and, in many cases, poorly marked. One standout exception is the ***Rainbow Trail***, a wilderness adventure for walking in the warm months and cross-country skiing in the winter. Hikers on the Rainbow Trail have the option of several short walks, or longer distances, as far as 5 miles. The main pathway wends its way across mostly even terrain, with open areas and some welcome shade, in the depths of the hardwood forests. There are several loops off the main trail, with the Sweetwater Loop, being the shortest at half a mile. There are unique environments to be found on the different loops. Noah's Nook is just off the main trail on the Solo Trail loop. The Wandering Wilderness Loop is somewhat rougher with elevation changes. At the very end of it all is the Cedar Haven down in the lowlands.

All along the way, songbirds will be around, making this a favorite for bird watchers. The wildflowers and the ground cover spread through the open areas attracting butterflies and hummingbirds. Open meadows, shady forest, wetlands, and an inland lake would be enough for most trails, but then there are those rainbows. Don't be surprised to see one. Rainbows are seen here all the time adding to the unique character of this trail. The loops are well marked, but the trail map available from the Visitors

Bureau or online, will be handy to have.

Local Treasures:

A very rare natural feature occurs on Drummond Island, known locally as the *Maxton Plains*. This flatland area is a unique grassland, called an alvar. Alvars are extremely rare plant communities, existing on limestone bedrock. Alvars are only found in parts of Canada, the United States and Sweden. These plains are grasslands, growing on very thin soil consisting of bulrush sedge and ragwort, prairie dropseed, prairie smoke, and Indian paintbrush. There are even fields of Prairie Smoke sprouting up through the cracks in the rocks. Another unusual feature of alvars, is that trees tend to grow in straight lines, following the soil filled cracks in the bed rock.

Another unusual feature on Drummond Island is the *Fossil Ledges*. The ledges are an outcropping on the north shore, where hikers can walk along the rocky shoreline. The shoreline is easily walk-able for about a mile. There is a large limestone outcropping near the trail, where there are several orange saltwater fossils. Picking up the broken stones along the shoreline will reveal all kinds of plant and animal fossils. The lake is beautiful here but remember that it drops off to a depth of more than 6o feet. Many varieties of wildlife can be found on the drive to the ledges and back. Some folks have even reported spotting a bear or two.

The rich history of the island has been preserved at the

Drummond Island Historical Museum. The museum is in a beautiful log building, housing artifacts and exhibits, depicting the history of the island. The fireplace was reconstructed from the stones of a chimney at Fort Drummond. There are Indian artifacts dating back to 200 B.C. A miniature of the British fort from the early 1800's is a favorite display. Then, there are writings and photos from the early 1900's about Maggie Walz, establishing a Finnish colony of at least 50 settlers on Homestead Grants. Unique exhibits include hand-tools, handicraft, pictures and memorabilia of the late 1800s and the early 1900s logging industry.

Directions:

The best thing you can do is get "the map" from the visitors center. Then take E. Maxton Rd. to S. Maxton Rd. Follow that to the Maxton Cut Across at the Maxton Plains. The trail head is less than 1/4 mile south of the intersection of Maxton Cut Cross Road and Maxton Road. Parking is available.

Important Notes:

The last stretch of S. Maxton Rd. and the Maxton Cut Across are gravel. There are no convenience facilities at the Rainbow Trail.

You will need specific directions to get to the Fossil Ledges. You can get directions online. The Ledges are north and east of the Four Corners in the same general direction as the Maxton Plains. From the Interpretive

Signs for the Maxton Plains to the Ledges involves about 45 minutes of travel. After crossing a swamp and traveling an old two track, one reaches the parking area.

First time visitors to Drummond Island are sometimes confused about where the "town" is. There really isn't one. There are several collections of businesses around different crossroads, each with its own attractions. "The Map" is invaluable for finding your way around the island and is available at most businesses.

Ringwood Forest Trails

Ringwood Forest is a rugged 160-acre park in the middle of Saginaw County. Within the three miles of trails, the *Historic Spruce Alley*, is one of the most beautiful loops, in a forest known for beauty. After a short walk through the grand evergreens of the Pine Promenade, the Spruce Alley, lined with towering pines more than a century old, winds through the woods and back to the banks of the Bad River. There are several main trails, in the Ringwood Forest, with loops through unique habitats branching off each one. The Walnut Ridge trail follows the course of the Bad River on the south bank. Board walks serve as bridges across small brooks. At the end of the main loop, is a scenic overlook of the river. From there hikers can take the Spruce Alley loop, or the Lumberjack loop, back to the picnic area. These same trails can be hiked in the opposite order by starting down the Pine Promenade. The Footbridge and Western trails are reached via the Muskrat Flats trail. This trail crosses the river, where it branches into the Witch Hazel loop and the Pine Hills Run loop. These are somewhat longer hikes, with the Witch Hazel long loop being almost 2 miles long. All of the main trails are just a few steps from the parking lot and picnic area.

This is a great place for nature lovers of all ages to enjoy the outdoors in all seasons. The trail loops, though unimproved, are conveniently short, most being under a half mile in length. The river and wetlands attract exotic birds, like mergansers and loons. There are places along the bank of the river for fishing. In the winter, these trails become cross-country ski trails. If you go in October, the Ringwood Forest will be a *riot of fall colors,* that will rival anything to be found "up north". The park has a pavilion available on a first come first serve basis, a picnic area, a playground, and pit toilets. The river access includes a canoe launch.

Local Treasures:

On the banks of the Shiawassee River, in Owosso, is one of the most distinctive historic structures anywhere in Michigan. The *Curwood Castle* is located in Curwood Castle Park, across the river from downtown Owosso. The building is a replica of a Norman chateau and was completed in 1923. It was used as a writing studio by James Oliver Curwood, a well known author of adventure novels. The castle is now a museum and is open to the public.

In 2002, a Hollywood film crew came to Owosso, Michigan to get authentic sounds and images of one of the biggest operating steam locomotives in the U.S. That 400+ ton giant became famous as the *Polar Express* in a movie by the same name. The train is housed at the Steam Railroading Institute in Owosso, and has been used for Christmastime passenger excursions since the late 1990's. This great old locomotive, the Pere Marquette 1225 almost ended up as scrap. Now it has become a holiday tradition.

A Bit of History:

The great pine forests in lower Michigan, were lumbered off by the mid 1860s. The trees in the Ringwood Forest, planted in the 1880s, are part of one of the first forest plantations established in Michigan.

Directions:

Ringwood Forest is located 2 miles South of St. Charles, about 15 miles north of Owosso, and 2 miles West of M-52 on Ring Road.

Important Notes:

The park has paved parking and an excellent sign with a map of the trails. From the parking area there is a fine paved pathway to a river overlook, adjacent to the picnic area, for the convenience of those unable to handle the unimproved forest trails.

THE

LANSING

SHOALS

LIGHTHOUSE

IS

VISIBLE

FROM

SCOTT'S

POINT

Scott's Point Beach Trail

The beach and shoreline at Scott's Point, are easy to get to, but are so little known that visitors often have the entire place to themselves. This spot is so secluded, that a walk along the beach could qualify as a "trail". I often use this shoreline trail as a break, on my drives across the upper peninsula, and have yet to see anyone else there. The road to Scott's Point, and the parking area are paved, yet when you exit your vehicle, the sense of seclusion is immediate. The only sounds are the waves of Lake Michigan, the whispering of the branches in the old forest, and songs of birds on the wing. The beach and the lake are just a few steps away.

A walk along the shoreline is an easy stroll on packed sand, that in some places extends well out into the lake, from there you get a view of the shoreline that is usually only possible from wading out into the water. At Scott's Point, the water is shallow in most places being only ankle deep more than 20 yards out. If you don't want to wade, there are usually a few long points of sand and pebbles that extend out into the water, formed by the action wind and water.

The beach can seem endless. From the parking area, the sand extends for more than a mile eastward along a gentle bay, past Peterson Point, visible in the distance. A few yards from the waterline the forest begins. Towering pines form a dense woodland, that is broken up by small ponds among the dunes, and several icy cold streams, that empty into the lake. The forest is home to the usual wildlife, out on the sand you may see Great Blue Herons, or Piping Plovers. Hidden away in the protection of the trees one can find a couple of rare wildflowers, the Lake Huron Tansy and the Dwarf Lake Iris.

Another feature of Scott's Point, that sparks the imagination, is the group of islands visible in the distance. The several islands, shimmering like a mirage on the surface of Lake Michigan, make up the Beaver Island Archipelago. On a clear day, one can even make out the abandoned lighthouse on Squaw Island. This is the closest view of the islands, from any spot on the Michigan mainland.

When you have had enough of the beach, and the sun, and the water, and the woods, and the solitude, there are some local treasures nearby.

Local Treasures:

Kitch-iti-Kipi (cold big water) or The Big Spring, was a sacred place to the native inhabitants of this area. One of the names they gave it was the "Mirror of Heaven". Kitch-iti-kipi is the largest spring in Michigan, at 300 feet by 175 feet. Fed by more than 20 springs, it is refreshed continuously with crystal-clear water. More than 10,000 gallons a minute gush up from the limestone bed.

Seul Choix Lighthouse, pronounced locally, Sis-Shwa and true French, Sel-Shwa) your "Only Choice" is a very beautiful lighthouse. Seul Choix Point was supposedly named by French sailors, who found that the protected bay, formed by the point was their "only choice" for shelter along that stretch of northern Lake Michigan's shoreline. Tower tours are available, and visitors are welcome to enjoy the surrounding grounds, which includes a picnic area.

The *Top of The Lake Snowmobile Museum*, in Naubinway, Michigan houses the biggest collection of Antique & Vintage Snowmobiles in the north. The museum is, "Where the history of snowmobiling comes to life".

Directions:

Getting to *Scott's Point* is easy. Take U.S. 2 west from the Mackinac Bridge, about 50 miles, or so, to Gould City. At the blinking light go south on Gould City Road. Though there is no sign, this is the road to Scott's Point which is just 9 miles away.

To visit *Kitch-iti-kipi,* travel west on US Hwy 2 from Manistique a couple of miles, turn onto M-149 north. Go 2.7 miles, then turn left to stay on M-149 north. Drive 1 mile, then turn right on County Road 455 (The sign says "Westshore - 455"). Drive 4.3 miles, then turn right on Sawmill Road and follow the signs to Palms Book State Park. It isn't as complicated as the directions sound.

To Visit the *Seul Choix Lighthouse*, go to Gulliver, Michigan, and follow the signs south.

Important Notes:

Scott's Point, while not particularly remote, has minimal facilities. As of 2017, the restrooms have been modernized and a nice pavilion has been installed. There are also excellent changing rooms for getting into that bathing suit. These improvements, along with picnic tables and grills, make this a nice picnic area.

Kitch-iti-kipi is inside Palm Book State Park, a fee is charged during the warm months.

Seul Choix Lighthouse is only open for tours during the summer months.

The *Snowmobile Museum* is in downtown Naubinway.

Seven Bridges Trail

When you get out of your car, the first thing you are aware of, is the sound of tumbling water. Just a few feet down the rustic path you come to the first bridge. By the time you pass the first bridge on the Seven Bridges Park Trail you will have left the everyday world behind and entered a world of tranquil natural beauty. Locally known as the "Jewel of Kalkaska County", the Seven Bridges Park is best known for its rustic wooden bridges that cross the Rapid River and its adjacent tributaries. The trail is only a mile long and is almost entirely forested. Along the streams and river, wildflowers will add their special beauty to the woodland scenery.

This river is a blue-ribbon trout stream, and the Seven Bridges area has over one mile of river frontage. It isn't unusual to encounter trout fishermen along the patchwork of interconnecting streams. The paths are nicely groomed, the boardwalks are well maintained, and the bridges are in excellent repair. While a few miles from anywhere, the music of the running water, the shaded pathways and profusion of wetland wildflowers, make this spot one of my favorite 15-minute vacations, while traveling the back roads. This level, one mile trail, is an easy stroll for most anyone.

Local Treasures:

Just west on Route 72, the *Cherry Street Market* is filled to bursting with fresh pure Michigan farm goods, locally grown products and lots of Michigan made goodies, the market is open May - November; locally owned and operated. Running for about a city block along the road front will be stacks of planters, flowers, fruits and vegetables, just begging you to stop for a quick look see. When you start wandering, it won't be long until you find the garden and statuary area in the back, and that area is enormous too. As if all this isn't enough, the market also operates a fantastic bakery/deli filled with delicious treats.

The Historical Museum has an *Elmer Car* on display. Elmer Johnson built bicycles for the Montgomery Ward Company and also built four cars, in his machine shop, on S. Cedar Street in Kalkaska. The car, known as the "Elmer", was built by hand in 1898 for Henry Stover, a druggist in Kalkaska.

Mountain Biker riders will want to head for the *Vasa Trail* that runs from Kalkaska to Acme. A recent upgrade with new markers and improvements have made this trail more rider-friendly for mountain bikers. This is a deep-woods trail, running through the Sand Lakes Quiet Area, along the same route used for the Iceman Cometh Race in November.

A Bit of History:

In the 1880s a sawmill was built, which dammed the Rapid River, creating a holding pond for logs. The remains of the dam can still be seen when crossing the first three bridges in Seven Bridges Park.

Directions:

Seven Bridges Park is east of Rapid City on Valley Rd. Valley Road is west of Kalkaska of Route 72.

The historical museum is located in the old railroad depot at Railroad Square.

Important Notes:

The parking area, for Seven Bridges, is just a gravel spot to pull off the side of the road. Kalkaska is the ***Mountain Bike Capital of Northern Michigan***. An information kiosk is to be located at Railroad Square.

KALKASKA

IS

A

STOP

ON

THE

ANNUAL

SPEEDER

CAR

TOUR

Sleepy Hollow North Trail

Northern Michigan around Charlevoix is famous for natural beauty, sparkling waters, and picturesque towns. During the summer months the population explodes with the return of tourists and summer residents. Everything is busy, even the nature areas can be bustling with people and traffic. In spite of the crowds, there are still places where quiet and solitude can be found. One of these is the Sleepy Hollow Nature Preserve, just north of East Jordan, on the west side of Lake Charlevoix. The easy trail there offers the opportunity for a break from the sometimes frantic pace of the busy towns.

Sleepy Hollow Nature Preserve covers a bit over 50 acres. The trail is only one mile long and that is split into two loops. Sear Creek is a spring fed stream that runs through the southern portion of the preserve. Don't let the short length of the trail fool you. This is a quiet preserve of dense forest. From the moment you go across the first bridge you will be in a beautiful nature area.

The first loop of the trail follows the course of Sear Creek for a way. There are nice benches scattered along the trail, providing places to pause, listen to the water and watch the wildlife that make this place their home. A number of simple boardwalks provide crossings where the trail meets the stream. It isn't unusual to spot brook trout in the clear water of the stream. There are some gentle hills with an elevation change of only about 80 feet throughout the entire preserve. The mix of maple, beech, aspen, and hemlock trees creates a fairly dense canopy. The result is cool shade along most of the pathway.

The second loop of the trail is found at the far end of the first loop and extends further into the forest. It is only a third of a mile long and loops back to the first trail. The second loop has another small elevation change. Large stumps can be found throughout the preserve, left overs from the lumbering days of the past. This nature preserve and trail are just a short distance from the towns, yet it isn't unusual to have the whole thing to yourself.

Local Treasures:

Ironton Ferry - If you are coming from the east, a very cool way to avoid some of the traffic, is a ride on the Ironton Ferry. The Ironton Ferry is a four-car cable ferry that crosses a narrow point on the South Arm of Lake Charlevoix. Back in the day, the Ironton Ferry was drawn by horses and most traffic was to serve the Pig Iron Factory in town.

It is more fun than one would expect. Getting to the ferry takes you through some gorgeous country. The ferry only holds four vehicles at a time and the whole trip takes about 2 minutes. The ferry runs between April and November. Captain Sam Alexander of the ferry is listed in "Ripley's Believe it or Not!" for traveling 15,000 miles while never being more than 1/4 mile from his home over a period of years.

Ironton is directly across from a parcel of land once owned by George R. Hemingway, uncle of renowned author Ernest Hemingway. "Uncle George" ran a tree farm on this property that includes a landmark on Lake Charlevoix, Hemingway Point. In Hemingway's, "The Nick Adams Stories", the point is where "Nick" was camping when he became frightened and fired rifle shots to signal his father and uncle who were out on the lake. This was confirmed by the author's first cousin, Margaret Hemingway Bundy, prior to her death.

Stone Hedge Gardens - Two acres of gardens are filled with gorgeous flower beds and decorative plantings. Water features, landscaping and garden art add to the beauty and serenity of the gardens.

According to the owners, "A unique touch of quality and design enlightens the space we've recreated inside our store". There are dozens of lotions, soaps, candles and those elusive one-of-a-kind finds. Taste the honey and locally baked goods. There is a huge variety of items for the home. You'll find kitchen ware, lamps, metal works, stained glass and a touch of shabby chic mixed with vintage antiques. Then there is the specialty jewelry, greeting cards, and an endless range of gifts for every occasion.

Elm Point Museum - Here is a really unusual museum in a really unusual setting. The museum is located on Elm Pointe where the Elm Pointe Estate is. It is okay to be confused when you first pull in, it looks just like you are pulling into someones driveway. I left twice and came back before I realized that this is the place.

On the grounds is the main residence and the lodge. On the main floor of the lodge is the East Jordan Portside Art and Historical Museum. This was the first established historical museum in Charlevoix County. Exhibits include stained glass, artifacts from the lumbering and fishing industries and the National Smelt Kings. Adjoining the museum is the Cygred Riley Art Gallery with its collection of works from the annual Portside Arts Fair.

Directions:

You have to watch for Sleepy Hollow Lane. The trailhead is quite secluded and is easily missed.

Turn east on Sleepy Hollow Lane off M-66 about half way between Charlevoix and East Jordan. Stay on Sleepy Hollow Lane for about 1/4 mile to the small parking area and trail head on the left.

Stone Hedge Gardens is located a bit north of the trail.

Elm Point Museum is 1.6 miles north of East Jordan.

Important Notes:

The parking area at the Sleepy Hollow trail head is tiny. There is room for only 3 or 4 vehicles making it tight for turning around.

Just south of Stone Hedge Gardens is Route C-48. Also known as the "Breezeway" this is a popular scenic drive.

ANDY T'S

IS

HOME

TO

THE

GIANT

PUMPKIN

CHAMPIONSHIPS

Sleepy Hollow Island Trail

Sleepy Hollow State Park, with more than 2,600 acres of prairie grasses, hardwood forest, and stands of pine trees, offers more multi-use trails than any other location near Lansing. A central feature of the park is Lake Ovid. The lake is quite shallow, covers over 400 acres, and has several small islands. Most of the trails in the park are located north of the lake, though one does sweep down the west side of the lake from the north. The main parking, camping, and recreation areas are all on the east side of the lake. Due to the layout of the parking and recreation areas, it is easy to miss one of the best short walks in the park, the *Sleepy Hollow Island Trail*.

The *Sleepy Hollow Island Trail* is the only trail in the park that takes hikers out to one of the islands in Lake Ovid. If you are at the main recreation area, where the beach and facilities are, it is a good long hike around the north end of the lake to the island trail spur. Then of course, you have to hike all the way back. There is another way that is much shorter, which makes it perfect for a nature walk, as part of a day trip. If you are approaching the park from U.S. 27 on Price Road, watch for a small sign indicating that, the boat launch entrance is a bit east of Shepardsville Road; take that entrance. At the curve just before the launch parking area, see a trail signpost marked with a large "L". That sign post leads to the island trail. If you park near the exit of the launch parking area, you will be away from all the boat launching activity, and only a short walk to the trail.

Back at the post with the large "L", you walk onto a wide two track trail, that is depicted on the map as a multi-use trail. You can walk that trail for less than half a mile, to reach the island trail spur, or you can take the small walking trail on the right, only a few steps from the "L" and enter a quiet forest path, that will ultimately take you to the bridge to the island. The forest trail option is beautiful, but it is a little rougher than the two track. The forest trail is also open to horses so you might encounter riders. It wanders through a variety of wildlife and mixed forest habitat. In early spring the wildflowers begin to peek through, and the "peepers" are raising a cacophony, in the ponds and wetlands. This trail winds around, roughly following the shoreline of the lake, though for most of the way you can't see the lake. About halfway there is an unusual pine tree on the right. Its' main trunk has somehow split into six sections or branches that have formed a bulb shape, where they split before growing straight up again. Another interesting tree is an ancient apple tree, sitting at the last curve in the trail before you reach an open area, and the bridge to the island.

At this point, the two trails meet at a fine pedestrian/horse bridge, that crosses over to the island. The bridge is quite short, maybe a hundred steps, and puts you directly on the island trail. There are three ways to explore the island, all of them are good. As you enter the great stand of trees, the trail goes straight ahead with a branch going north and another branch going south. If you continue straight, the trail goes through the giant maples and beeches, directly across the island to the shoreline of the lake. This spot offers views of the lake and some of the other islands. On the other hand, taking the north or south branches, will lead to two entirely different environments. The north branch follows the shoreline around the island through a primarily, hardwood forest. The south branch also follows the shoreline, but very quickly takes you into a stand of enormous pines. Walking through the pine scented air with the wind gusting through the tree tops, is just like being in one of the great pine forests "up north". Whatever option is chosen, the entire walk around the island will take less than half an hour, and then it is less than half an hour back to the boat launch parking. This is a gorgeous walk, and it can be quite crowded on weekends, when the park is full. Almost any other time, you could have it all to yourself. The variety of trees, flowers, birds, and wildlife make this an entertaining place to take a walk with the kids.

Local Treasures:

Wildlife – At last count, in 2014, over 228 different animal species have been identified in Sleepy Hollow State Park. Along with the song birds and the waterfowl of all kinds, bird watchers have spotted rare birds, such as, Bonaparte's gull and bald eagles.

The Great Pumpkin – About ten minutes from the park you can wander through the flowers and gardens at Andy T's. In late autumn this is the collection point for the biggest pumpkins produced by growers all over the region. At the same time, you can try your hand at sending pumpkins flying across the fields, with the **Pumpkin Sling Shot**. Some "slingers" go for distance and some go for accuracy. It doesn't really matter it is just plain fun for kids and adults. Andy T's prides itself on offering the freshest produce and uses the best environmentally-friendly practices to grow award winning and nationally recognized vegetables, plants, trees, and flowers. Over the years, Andy T has been known for his famous **Gourmet Sweet Corn,** that has been shipped all over the planet! Be sure to say hello to Andy and the staff, they helped make this chapter possible.

On the other side of St. Johns, is a company called AgroLiquid. Inside the headquarters building is one of the most unique activity centers in all of Michigan. The **"Iqhub",** is described as an agriculture activity center. It is certainly that, and it is a whole lot more. This is a really fun place for the kids. Within the 9,400 square feet of space are 24 museum-quality exhibits that depict agricultural history and practices in the Americas, from the time Europeans first arrived here, up to the present day. The **"IQhub"** is an educational adventure that teaches children and adults alike, the farm-to-fork connection of the foods we find in our markets.

Everybody is going to have fun in this place, partly because it is hands on and partly because everybody who comes here will learn something new. Unique exhibits include a bone grinder, the Law of the Minimum demonstration, and a virtual tractor to play with. The bone grinder works. This simple machine was used to grind up animal bones to release the phosphates to be used as fertilizer. This might be the only working bone grinder on display in the state. The Law of the Minimum teaches the importance of nutrient balance when fertilizing your plants. The virtual tractor exhibit is easily the most popular in the center. You get to climb into the cockpit of a giant modern tractor and take it for a spin around the farm. Kids often have to wait, until their dads and uncles are finished playing, to get a turn on the tractor.

There is another treasure nearby, in downtown St. Johns. The *Historic Grand Trunk Depot* building serves as the Clinton Northern Railway Museum. Railroad enthusiasts can find rail cars from the early 1900s, with a focus on Barney and Smith Cars. In addition to the rail cars, there are collections of railroad artifacts and memorabilia.   A favorite is the four seasons model train layout in the east room of the Depot.

Directions:

Sleepy Hollow State Park - Take US-27 north of I-69, to the Price Road exit. Go east about 5.5 miles. The Park entrance is on the north side of road.

Andy T's – Take US-27 north from Price Road for three miles. Great pumpkin is on the east side.

IQ HUB - 1130 S. Dewitt Rd, Saint Johns, MI 48879 at the corner of M-21 and Dewitt Road in Saint Johns, Michigan in the AgroLiquid Headquarters.

Grand Trunk Depot – North end of downtown St. Johns at the railroad tracks across from the library.

Important Notes:

Sleepy Hollow State Park requires an entrance fee. There is a vault toilet at the boat launch parking area. There are no facilities on or near the island, except a place to hitch your horse.

Andy T's is closed during the winter months. The railroad depot is open Sundays 1-3 in the summer.

Admission is free at the The "Iqhub".

Southern Links Trailway

The "thumb" area of Michigan is sometimes called, the "forgotten digit" of the mitten. Amid the broad fields of this vast agricultural region, are trails and treasures, unlike any in the rest of the state. Those looking for a place to take a walk, and enjoy the wildlife, might want to try the pathway known as the ***Southern Links Trailway***.

While there are water trails and bicycle routes in the region, the Southern Links Trailway has a lot to offer for hikers, bikers and walkers on snow shoes of all skill levels. This rail-trail runs 10-miles through the communities of Columbiaville, Otter Lake, and Millington, just south of Caro. The trail is paved with smooth asphalt, an adjacent path is offered for those who prefer to travel on horseback. On a bicycle, you could just coast from Otter Lake to Millington because of the gentle incline from the old railroad days when this was the Detroit and Bay City Railway.

The ten foot wide paved surface is especially suited to groups who like to ride bikes together. A variety of deciduous trees line the trail and the colors are spectacular in the fall months. Trail users will pass through a mixed rural landscape, including fields, wetlands, forests and farmland. Local wildlife is plentiful including rabbits, chipmunks, woodchucks, frogs and turtles. Encounters between the animals and trail users are not uncommon. The southern section of the trail is popular with bird watchers.

Local Treasures:

The ***Octagon Barn,*** is in nearby Gagetown. This is easily the most unusual barn anywhere in the region. It is the largest timber frame octagon barn in the country, at 102 feet across and 70 feet high. When construction began in 1924, it was known as an air castle, because the entire vast interior is open, and the roof seems to be suspended above. What exists on this site today is the result of a vision, a team effort, generous contributions, and many hours of planning, organization and plain hard work. The vision began in the minds of a few neighbors, who did not want to see such an awesome structure and piece of agricultural history be destroyed, in the name of 'convenience' or 'progress'.

Shopping - Take a break from the trail in Millington and head downtown. There are several ***small antique stores*** and a wonderful country store loaded with home decor, candles and gifts!

If you don't mind a short drive, head to the Capac Historical Museum, where the "***Mechanical Wonder of the Ages***", is on display. This is a model city remarkable for its size and detail. When fully functioning it looks like an actual living city. Lights inside most of the structure reveal that life in "Model City" is not restricted to the streets. A man rocks comfortably in a chair inside the Maxwell Coffee House, and a new fire engine is poised inside the doors of the fire station. Blue lights flash on and off at the welding factory indicating a night shift at work. A general store on the main drag displays bananas and other fresh fruit. All the more remarkable is the fact that the whole thing runs on small sewing machine motors and belts, no transistors and no computer chips. It is a great thing to preserve; I can't see how one could be built from scratch today.

Directions:

Parking for the *Southern Links Trailway* is available at trail heads in Columbiaville on Water Street; Otter Lake on Detroit Street; and Millington at the school complex on Gleason Street.

Octagon Barn - Drive about a mile east of the Village of Gagetown along the Bay City Forestville Road. Go north on Richie Road.

Important Notes:

The Southern Links Trailway is a multi-use trail, so walkers may be sharing the pathway with bikers, skaters, and even horses.

SOME

CALL

THE

STURGEON

RIVER

GORGE

THE

GRAND

CANYON

OF

MICHIGAN

Sturgeon River Gorge Trail

This trail is more challenging than most. The roaring waters at the bottom of the gorge will make it all worth it. It is no accident that some people refer to this spot as the "*Grand Canyon*" of Michigan.

This is an incredibly beautiful area but the trail down into the gorge is quite narrow and can be treacherous. In fact, the wall of the gorge is so steep that the trail uses a series of switchbacks to deal with the steep canyon walls. Switchbacks or not, sections of the trail are still quite steep and very slippery when the ground is wet and muddy. This is an unimproved trail with rocks and tree roots along the way. Make sure you have proper footwear, like no flip flops, and a walking stick might be come in handy. You have a long descent. It would be around 400 feet if you were going straight down. Still, it isn't extreme. Our group was all people over 70 years of age and we had no problems.

The series of waterfalls at the bottom of the trail make it all worth it. You may even forget that you have to climb back out. You find yourself on a wide flat area of bedrock perhaps fifteen to twenty feet above the river facing a small waterfall. As you work your way along the trail both upstream and down, there are several falls and cataracts. One will be a fairly, gentle rapids and another will be a turbulent cataract crashing through steep canyon walls throwing clouds of mist into the air. Getting the really cool photographs involves some work. In one place you have to climb down a steep trail. In another you are down in the canyon with the water roaring through just a couple feet away. Everywhere you step you are on wet slippery rocks or slick ground with roots protruding. Taking your time, being careful will result in a wonderful experience at a spot that many people never locate.

There are no facilities, and you may be off the grid. This is a genuine wilderness so be prepared. Take water and you might want a trail snack as well. It is a long way down to the river and it takes some effort to make it back up especially if you go in the summer and must contend with heat, mosquitoes, and black flies. It is worth every bit of it.

Directions - The best way to get there is go west out of L'Anse on Route 38 toward Ontonagon to Baraga Plains Rd. Go south and find Clear Creek Rd. Take that road for several miles through the forest to reach the *Sturgeon River Gorge Wilderness* and the trailhead. These roads are gravel much of the way.

Thornapple River Trail

The Paul Henry-Thornapple Trail, in west Michigan, is under development. One of the best completed sections, for a quiet afternoon, is the ***Thornapple River Walk*** in Hastings, Michigan. The walk is a paved pathway, that runs a mile and a half along the Thornapple River with loop trails at each end. One end is in Bliss Riverfront Park, and the other end, is in Tyden Park. Tyden Park, has plenty of parking and a few picnic tables, making it a good place to start, for a trails and treasures day trip.

First, there is the walk along the Thornapple River itself. Where you park, the pathway is only steps away, and there are map signs right at hand, so you know where you are. Follow the course of the river, and you will be treated to all of the natural beauty that the Thornapple River Valley is known for. If you don't want to walk the full distance to the Bliss Riverfront Park, take the foot bridge across the river, and enter a network of groomed trails that meander through the trees and wildflowers.

This is the loop at the Tyden Park end of the trail, and it is worth going to the park just to wander around in this tiny wilderness, on the edge of town. As soon as you cross the bridge, turn left, and you will be in the trails. One part follows the course of the river, and others branch off, looping into a maze of trees, shrubs, and wildflowers. At one junction, there is an enormous Sycamore tree, that is so large you can't get your arms all the way around it. The canopy of trees and dense undergrowth are home to a wide range of waterfowl and songbirds. Another interesting feature here, is the fantastic number of tiny gossamer webs to be found at ground level. They are usually nearly invisible, but if you come while the dew is still on the ground, you can see dozens glistening in the early morning sunlight.

Local Treasures:

For a decade, *AlFresco Suites,* has offered exceptional quality and service to hundreds of suite guests. Conveniently located two blocks from the Waldorff Banquet facility, it is a local favorite for wedding guests, as well as local corporations. Guests enjoy comfort, security, privacy, and downtown convenience. Below the luxury rooms is the shop featuring unique, quality gifts. Stop in, browse, and thank them for sponsoring this chapter.

Only two blocks from the trail at Tyden Park, is the *Sculpture Walk,* in downtown Hastings. It all started with one statue in 2009. Now there are twenty pieces, and more are planned. A local favorite is "Procession", in front of City Hall. The piece is the work of award-winning Williamston artist, Mark Chatterley. Large ceramic female figures carry a male figure, representing a "dream time" journey. Along the sidewalks and parks, spaces as utilitarian as parking lots, are enlivened with metallic horses, bronze girls, book-reading frogs, birds in flight, and many abstract shapes.

All of this hiking and shopping can work up an appetite. Of all the options in town, we keep returning to *Kloosterman's,* right next to AlFresco. They call it a sports tap and grille which is accurate. That doesn't begin to tell you how good the food and service are. Their burgers and steaks are always cooked just exactly the way you want them.

The historic *Charlton Park Village and Museum,* has been a tradition in Barry County since 1936, and is often referred to as the "jewel of Barry County." Situated on more than 300 acres along the Thornapple Lake, the recreation area offers many options for outdoor activities including hiking, boating, swimming, and fishing.

A Bit of History:

The Paul Henry-Thornapple Trail, became possible when the Michigan Central Railroad sold portions of its right-of-way, to the State of Michigan and Rails-to-Trails. The Thornapple Trail Association joined in, and the trail development began. Eventually, there will be about 42 miles of multi-use trail.

TROY

IS

WHERE

THE

WOODCOCK

DANCE

HAPPENS

EACH

SPRING

Troy Nature Trails

When thinking about a nature getaway and beautiful trails, many people automatically think about a trip "up north". Northern Michigan is famous for natural beauty, unspoiled wilderness, and hiking trails everywhere. However, excellent nature areas, well developed trails, and Michigan wildlife are sometimes close at hand, even in metropolitan areas. The trails, and natural beauty, found at the Stage Nature Center in Troy, Michigan, are a perfect example of these urban treasures.

The trails start immediately outside the visitors center. These are primarily wood chip trails that are wide and well shaded. The trail system is divided in to a number of loops and winds through about 100 acres. There is variety of wildlife here, due to the diversity of habitats, including forest, meadow, marsh, pond and stream. In fact, the streams here are the headwaters of the Rouge River. The trail loops are easy walks, accessible to nearly everyone.

The longest loop, the ***Blackbird Loop***, is less than 3/4 of a mile in length. It includes a boardwalk that passes through a wet forest, a dry meadow, a climax forest, and a wet sedge meadow. This mix of habitats is home to a broad range of plant life that attracts birds galore.

The ***Sugar Maple Loop*** is less than 1/2 mile long. It winds through a low, wet forest. Growing along the way are musclewood, skunk cabbage, and old American elms. When the trail moves into a dryer area, there are sugar maples, beeches, and red oak.

The *Bluebird Loop* is quite short, in fact, it functions as a short cut for the Blackbird Loop. The trail pathway defines the edge between a forest and field. This habitat is home to an amazing variety of animals.

Then there is the *Fox Loop*, again, less than 1/2 mile long. Lots of different natural features are found on this trail including some created by human disturbance. There is a short side trail that leads to the "Marsh Tower" From there one gets an excellent view of the bottom lands of the Rouge River. This is also the trail that leads to a clearing where the annual dance of the woodcock occurs.

Local Treasures

Stage Nature Center - The visitors center contains classrooms, a public research library, an observation bee hive, a wildlife viewing area and a nature exhibition lobby. The headwaters of the Rouge River flow through the 100-acre preserve. More than 145 plant and animal species can be viewed throughout the grounds. An outdoor natural play area features climbing boulders, and a paved path that provides wheelchair access to the stream side forest. Within the nature center are over 1.5 miles of trails, which pass through upland forest, meadows, stream side wetlands, and a cattail marsh.

The nature preserve is a valuable community asset offering a quiet retreat to solitary observers, couples, Scout groups, families, and school children who come to enjoy the natural beauty of the preserve. Some people come to sit on a bench, some to count bluebirds - others test water quality, monitor pond life, or tap the sugar maples. Many take the opportunity to capture photos of the wildlife for their own use and to enhance the society's marketing initiatives.

Monarch Butterfly Way Station - Way Station #15682

In the fall, hundreds of millions of monarch butterflies migrate from the United States and Canada to overwintering areas in Mexico and California. There they wait out the winter until conditions favor a return flight in the spring. The monarch migration is truly one of the world's greatest natural wonders, yet it is threatened by habitat loss in North America - at the overwintering sites, and throughout the spring and summer breeding range as well.

Monarch Waystations are places that provide resources necessary for monarchs to produce successive generations and sustain their migration. Without milkweeds throughout their spring and summer breeding areas in North America, monarchs would not be able to produce the successive generations that culminate in the migration each fall.

Dance of the Woodcock - Every spring the male woodcock performs his courtship dance. He comes out into a forest opening, bog, or power line cut. Open sky is important because the dance takes place high in the air. Just after sunset, the woodcock begins to circle making a "peeent" sound. Soon he begins to ascend and the "peeent" sound is replaced by a twittering sound. High in the sky the woodcock circles round and round. The twitter becomes faster as the pace of the dance quickens and is replaced by a loud chirping. Then the chirping stops, and the bird comes sloping back down to his "peeenting" location. The Dance of the Woodcock takes place every year, usually in the last two weeks of April.

Troy Historic Village - The story of southeast Michigan is told through buildings, artifacts and programs at the Troy Historic Village. The village contains eleven 19th and early 20th-century buildings. Visitors can explore three different homes, a general store, wagon shop, and many others, all from the mid-1800s to the early turn-of-the-century. Volunteers built a forge and installed bellows from the 1700s. Students learn traditional blacksmith skills and create forged art during Artisan classes. This is a great place for children, but pets are not allowed.

Directions:

The Stage Nature Center is located at 6685 Coolidge Highway in Troy, Michigan.

Union Mine Trail

Don't let the name put you off. This isn't a dark and damp underground path through an old abandoned mine. This is an easy trail, about one mile, that loops back to the parking area. The winding trail through the towering trees is shady and cool. Along the way are interpretive signs, old ruins, and waterfalls, and there is no steep climb back to the top. While it isn't paved or groomed, the trail is in good condition and can be walked by most anyone.

The beginning of the trail is clearly marked, with an informative sign and a giant shovel. Along the trail are more of these interpretive signs describing what a casual hiker might not notice. The trail is pleasant, though it seems unremarkable at first. Then you come to the stream that tumbles down the slope, sparkling in the sunlight. The pathway follows the cascading stream leading to ruins and artifacts of the mining activity that took place here. There is a rectangular cut in the bed of the stream, that creates a small waterfall. That cut is man-made and had a water wheel mounted in it. The water wheel only produced a couple of horsepower, but the miners wanted to use it to hoist waste rock and ore up out of the mine shaft. There is a long trench that was dug out of the living rock to locate the vein of copper, numerous mine shafts, and the remnants of the old Nonesuch Road. The Nonesuch, was the first road into this region. They called it a road, but it was so rough and full of holes, that it was suggested you lash yourself to your wagon, to avoid being pitched out onto your head.

Fortunately, the Union Mine Trail is nothing like that. Most of it is a natural trail, but it is smooth and easy to walk. The mine shafts are fenced off, so the puppy dog won't fall in, and even the way back is pretty easy. Rather than a steep climb back up, the trail rises gently with a few short sets of stairs to help along the way.

Local Treasures:

Bonanza Falls - If you follow Route 64, south out of Silver City, you will arrive at Bonanza Falls in just a few minutes. Watch carefully for the small sign on the west side of the road. The road from the sign to the falls is gravel, but it is only a hundred yards or so. You could park and walk. At the end of that short road is another parking area, and just through the trees is Bonanza Falls. This is a great place for a short break or a picnic. The river, only a few feet from the parking area, is broad and gentle. The falls are a series of cascades and cataracts, broken up by wide flat areas of bed rock. Lots of folks walk out and find a wide flat dry area to sit and enjoy the sun and water. A really great place and easy to get to for anyone.

Tales of fabulous silver deposits have been around since the earliest days of exploration in the upper peninsula. Silver mixed, but unalloyed with native copper, known as "free silver", has been brought out of the copper mines. The legends grew since most of the silver was smuggled out of the mines, in the miners' dinner pails.

One silver deposit did exist near the Iron River, just inland from Lake Superior. Bonanza Falls was named by Austin Corser, in honor of his discovery of a rich pocket of silver ore in 1855. He kept this discovery secret for seventeen years, because he couldn't file a claim until a government land grant for a proposed railroad expired, in 1872. Once the discovery became public the "silver rush" was on, including the establishment of the nearby town of Silver City. Early assays came in between $185.00 to $1,716.00 per ton. Unfortunately, the first silver ingot refined from the ore, came out at $33.00 per ton. The upshot was, that it would cost more to mine the silver, than it was worth. The "silver rush" was over by 1876. Then the lumber companies arrived. The Greenwood Lumber Company, flourished for a while beginning in 1908, and the waterfall became known as Greenwood Falls. A forest fire wiped out most of the buildings in 1921, and now there are no buildings remaining, nature has reclaimed everything. In 1998, this spot was named a heritage site.

Lake of the Clouds - The Lake of the Clouds, is located inside the Porcupine Mountains State Park, near Ontonagon, Michigan. Several hundred acres of old growth forest, surround this incredible treasure. A short hike from the parking area, will take you to spots where you can enjoy the spectacular view. At any time of year this spot will inspire the artist and nature lover in all of us. The lake is a prominent feature of the park, and a favorite "up north" Michigan attraction. The lake is fed from the east end by the Carp River Inlet, and the outflow from the western end is the Carp River, which empties into Lake Superior, on the boundary between Ontonagon and Gogebic County. The Lake of the Clouds may be the most photographed lake in all of Michigan.

Ontonagon Lighthouse - The Ontonagon Lighthouse, has been fully restored and is operated by the Ontonagon County Historical Society. The lighthouse is open six days a week. Tours begin at the Museum complex downtown, then move out to the lighthouse complex, and culminate in the lantern room at the top. From that spot visitors have a great view of the lake, harbor, and the unique profile of the Porcupine Mountains, 20 miles distant. The stories and details that are included in the tour make it a real treat.

By a happy coincidence, it was discovered that a lantern suspended from the steeple of a Church, located high atop a hill at the town of Rockland, 12 miles inland, could be seen from some distance out on Lake Superior. By lining up the Church light with the Ontonagon Lighthouse, ships could steer straight into the Harbor at night!

In October 1975, the Ontonagon Lighthouse was placed on the National Register of Historic Places.

A Bit of History:

1846 saw the beginning of the first "mineral rush" in America. Like the "gold rush" that came later, the rush to Michigan's "Copper Country" attracted men from every background, speculators, scientists, miners and desperadoes. Most of the miners who came didn't really expect riches, they just needed a better way to make a living. The discovery, or rediscovery, of major copper deposits in Michigan represented a genuine chance to get ahead for anyone who could handle the difficult work. Michigan is the only place in the world where economically abundant deposits of pure, elemental copper are found on or near the surface, as well as deep underground. A mine could be started with nothing more than a pick and a shovel.

The Union Copper Company opened in 1846 and provided employment for some of these men. The pay was about $40.00 per month, and each miner was allowed to kill as many black flies as he wanted. The mine closed the following year but reopened for a few years when the war between the states broke out, and the demand for metals of all kinds increased dramatically.

To give you an idea of working conditions, a tunnel about 70 feet long connects Shaft #1 and Shaft #2. That tunnel goes under the river. It was constructed using sledgehammers, picks and hand drills, with a little black powder thrown in. The only light in these tunnels was provided by candles. Tons of waste rock and water had to be dragged out by hand. There is more detail available along the trail.

Directions:

Union Mine Trail - Route 64 West from Ontonagon will become the 107th Engineers Memorial Highway at Silver City, continue west toward the Porcupine Mountains. As you approach the Porkies, see the South Boundary Road, which leads to the Visitors Center. Stay on the South Boundary Road for a couple of miles and watch for the trail head on the west side of the road.

Important Notes:

The short drive to the Union Mine trail head is not paved. Maps and information are available at the Visitors Center just around the corner. Pets should be on a leash this is a wilderness.

Wilderness Arboretum Trail

The Wilderness Arboretum, in Port Austin, Michigan, is a place where the natural environment is protected for scientific and educational purposes. Back in the day, local kids call it "The Woods", where they could explore dry forests and wetlands. The Arboretum is home to all manner of native Michigan plants and animals, birds and wildflowers protected by shallow wetlands, and sandy ridges extending to the nearby beach. This beautiful nature center has a number of easy to walk, well maintained trails, including handicapped access trails. The wilderness arboretum encompasses over 100 acres of natural beauty, convenience facilities and a Visitor Center.

The paved handicapped accessible trail is a walk into the giant oak trees and an amazing variety of wildflowers. The trail leads to one of the few dry swales found in this region, a forested ridge, and eventually, onto a boardwalk that leads to an interdunal wetland.

The longer trails are mostly improved with wood chips and will take hikers to that same dry swale and a wooded ridge habitat. These trails will also wind through moist woods and wetlands, as well as stands of hardwoods. Boardwalks are provided in particularly wet areas. There are benches along the way where nature lovers can rest, or simply pause, to drink in the pure forest air. This type of wooded environment once covered the entire thumb.

If all this weren't enough, the Wilderness Arboretum is home to a Lady Slipper Festival every Memorial Day weekend. In years past, the high point of the festival, was the discovery of more than 100 of the rare Pink Lady's Slipper Orchid.

Local Treasures:

For a gorgeous view of Lake Huron, stop in at Lisa's Loft in the historic brick building at the corner of Lake and Spring Streets above Heins Hardware in downtown Port Austin. The view is truly breathtaking. Besides offering the view, Lisa's is a fantastic gift shop. The fine selection of everyday gifts and seasonal items, includes works by local artists. Add in the variety of antiques and vintage items, jewelry, books, journals, cards, nautical and cottage items, and you will understand why we are proud to have Lisa's as our sponsor.

Port Austin is one of the few places where you can watch the sun rise over a Great Lake and watch it set over a Great Lake. Crescent State Park on the beach has a five-mile long hiking trail, and there is the "Tip of the Thumb Heritage Water Trail" for kayakers and canoeists. One of the favorite water destinations is Turnip Rock.

Then there is the Port Austin Lighthouse, which was occupied by a keeper until 1953, when it was automated. It is one and a half to two and a half miles from shore, depends on who you ask, off the tip of the Michigan

"Thumb", resting on the reef that it marks. The water is as shallow as 3 feet in some places, and it is clear enough to see the dangerous rocks below. Nearby you can find the Thumb Area Bottomland Preserve, where divers explore offshore caves and the remains of shipwrecks.

A Bit of History:

The first salt well in Huron County, was sunk at Port Austin, Michigan in 1864. Brine was struck at a depth of 1,184 feet. The salt made here took the first prize at the state fair in Ohio and was considered the finest made in Michigan.

Directions:

For the Wilderness Arboretum, from Port Austin, go west on M-25 to Oak Beach and turn south on Oak Beach Road. Loosemore Road will be on your left, turn down Loosemore and the Nature Center will be on the left about 1/4 mile.

Important Notes:

The Wilderness Arboretum trails are open year-round (dawn to dusk) and are free to the public. Loosemore Road is gravel.

THE

BIG

CEDAR

IS

JUST

A

FEW

MILES

FROM

DOWNTOWN

MIO

Wolf Creek Trail

The Wolf Creek Trail winds through different environments with several loops providing options for longer or shorter walks. The trail, a mix of groomed gravel and boardwalks, twists and turns through a large section of prime land along the AuSable River. The forests here are cedar, oak, and pine that make up the Huron-Manistee National Forest. The trail access is at the Au Sable River public access site just a couple of blocks from downtown Mio. The trail begins right at the paved parking area and follows the course of the river. Within a short distance an excellent boardwalk takes hikers through wetlands and wildflowers to a small bridge that crosses Wolf Creek. The variety and convenience provided, make this a favorite trail, for those looking for a short break in a forested semi-primitive setting.

This first section of the trail offers several spots where hikers can pause beside the pristine waters of the Au Sable River. The first loop is less than half a mile from the trail head. From that junction the trail creates a short loop and intersects further on with other junctions where longer hikes can be taken. Along the way are interpretive signs that describe habitats and history. In addition to views of the river, trail users can observe a wide diversity of plants in a natural woodland setting and can expect to encounter a variety of wildlife. The entire trail system is non-motorized and covers just under five miles.

Local Treasures:

The Orion International Dark Sky Park, in the Bull Gap area near Mio, will be the first in the nation to be certified inside a National Forest. The Bull Gap trail head has a parking area and restrooms. There is an open area at that trail head, which is perfect for night sky viewing, photography and for setting up telescopes for viewing planets and constellations. The International Dark Sky Association (IDA) recently added two more Dark Sky Parks, taking the number of officially recognized star-gazing spots around the world to 25.

The gorgeous *Au Sable River* runs through Mio, Michigan, on its way to Lake Huron. In French, au sable literally means "with sand." A 1795 map calls it the Beauais River. The stretch of the Au Sable River from Grayling to Lake Huron offers breathtaking scenery as well as excellent wildlife viewing opportunities. Panoramic vistas from high bluff overlooks, long wooden boardwalks over spring-fed streams and miles of quiet, undeveloped shoreline all can be found along this scenic river. The Au Sable River is considered one of the best brown trout fisheries east of the Rockies, and has been designated a blue ribbon trout stream by the Michigan Department of Natural Resources.

The *Our Lady of the Woods Shrine* is an enormous limestone structure, honeycombed with grottoes and niches. The shrine is actually several shrines, each with a different purpose, all woven together. The shrine is open to all. Visitors are encouraged to stop and explore the statuary and dedications. It began with the visions of Rev. Hubert Rakowski in the mid 40's and was dedicated in September of 1955.

The *Big Cedar* is one of the largest native white cedar trees on the mainland of Michigan. It is more than 150 inches around with a diameter in excess of 47 inches, almost 4 feet. The total height is over 40 feet. A storm sometime in the past removed a large part of the original crown about 29 feet above the ground. The break at that point has a diameter of more than two feet.

No one is sure of the exact age of the big cedar but estimates put it at more than 350 years old. That would mean that it was just a little seedling or small sapling when the Pilgrims landed at Plymouth Rock. The tree is in a sort of loop of the Au Sable River which may explain how it survived the forest fires of the early 1900s. The lumberjacks probably gave it a pass because of its defects.

A Bit of History:

Mio had one of the earliest public water systems in Northern Michigan. First constructed in 1890 water was pumped from Wolf Creek through a 4 inch wooden pipe to a hilltop reservoir south of town. A six inch wooden main then ran down hill along M-33 all the way to M-72. Smaller pipes then branched off to serve water customers.

Directions:

The second **Wolf Creek** public access point is 2.0 miles east of the stop light on County Road 602. This access point and parking lot are the best spot for winter sport activities.

The **Orion International Dark Sky** Park is 5 miles east of Mio on 8th st./South River Rd. also known as County Road 602.

The **Big Cedar** is on U.S Forest land east of Mio, Michigan. Go east from the light in Mio on 8th St. for 2.5 miles to Forest Road 4354, go north for about 1.5 miles to an intersection, then left into the parking area for the tree or right to get to parking for the fishing area.

Important Notes:

The parking area at the Orion International Dark Sky Park is gravel and is adjacent to the Bull Gap trail system that is primarily used by ORV enthusiasts.

Trail Map Notes

This book does not contain detailed trail maps. Trail conditions change often, due to natural changes, man made improvements, and other factors.

Up to date maps are usually available locally or online.

Notes:

Notes:

Notes:

Notes:

Notes:

Notes:

Notes:

Notes:

Notes: